THE
GREEN
SEA OF
HEAVEN

30TH ANNIVERSARY EDITION

THE GREEN SEA OF HEAVEN

80 Ghazals from the Díwán of Háfiz

TRANSLATED BY
ELIZABETH T. GRAY, JR.
& IRAJ ANVAR

AFTERWORD BY
DARYUSH SHAYEGAN

Monkfish Book Publishing Company
Rhinebeck, New York

The Green Sea of Heaven: 80 Ghazals from the Díwán of Háfiz © copyright 2024 by Elizabeth T. Gray, Jr., and Iraj Anvar

All rights reserved. No part of this book may be used or reproduced in any manner without the consent of the publisher except in critical articles or reviews. Contact the publisher for information.

Paperback ISBN 978-1-958972-35-9
eBook ISBN 978-1-958972-36-6

Library of Congress Cataloging-in-Publication Data

Names: Ḥāfiẓ, active 14th century, author. | Gray, Elizabeth T., 1952- translator. | Anvar, Iraj, translator. | Shayegan, Darius, writer of afterword. | Ḥāfiẓ, active 14th century. Dīvān. Selections. English. | Ḥāfiẓ, active 14th century. Dīvān. Selections.
Title: The green sea of heaven : 80 ghazals from the Díwán of Háfiz / translated by Elizabeth T. Gray, Jr. & Iraj Anvar ; afterword by Daryush Shayegan.
Description: 30th anniversary edition. | Rhinebeck, New York : Monkfish Book Publishing Company, 2024. | Includes bibliographical references. | English and Persian.
Identifiers: LCCN 2024031675 (print) | LCCN 2024031676 (ebook) | ISBN 9781958972359 (paperback) | ISBN 9781958972366 (ebook)
Subjects: LCSH: Ḥāfiẓ, active 14th century--Translations into English. | LCGFT: Poetry.
Classification: LCC PK6465.Z32 G73 2024 (print) | LCC PK6465.Z32 (ebook) | DDC 891/.5511--dc23/eng/20240801
LC record available at https://lccn.loc.gov/2024031675
LC ebook record available at https://lccn.loc.gov/2024031676

Book and cover design by Colin Rolfe

Monkfish Book Publishing Company
22 East Market Street, Suite 304
Rhinebeck, NY 12572
(845) 876-4861
monkfishpublishing.com

*For Chip and Farrokh
Sam and William
Hedieh, Hatam, and Sina*

CONTENTS

Preface to the 30th Anniversary Edition
ix

Preface to the 2019 Edition
xi

Preface to the 1995 Edition
xiii

Note on Transliteration
xv

Translators' Introduction
xvii

The Ghazals
1

Afterword: The Visionary Topography of Háfiz, by Daryush Shayegan
167

Notes to the Ghazals
187

Selected Bibliography
231

About the Translators
239

PREFACE TO THE 30TH EDITION

It has now been thirty years since Steve Scholl and White Cloud Press brought fifty of these translated ghazals into the world. We are deeply grateful to Paul Cohen and the team at Monkfish Book Publishing for urging us to prepare this 30th Anniversary Edition, and for welcoming the Persian originals back into the text. We have taken this opportunity to walk through, once again, every ghazal, line by line, querying and refining our prior work and being dazzled—again—by Háfiz's genius.

Happily, since 1995, the amount of scholarship and translation available to the English reader, on Háfiz and other classical Persian poets, has grown enormously. The ghazal form has become familiar, and has been embraced by poets writing in English.

We hope that these poems will continue to inspire and give pleasure to readers, writers, and students who are familiar with Háfiz, and to those who are meeting him for the first time.

ELIZABETH T. GRAY JR. AND IRAJ ANVAR
NEW YORK CITY AND BARRINGTON, RHODE ISLAND
JANUARY 2024

PREFACE TO THE 2019 EDITION

Twenty-five years ago, Iraj and I spent most afternoons at a dining room table in New York City, arguing over lines of Háfiz, as he helped me finalize my translations of Iran's great poet. In the intervening decades we have continued to learn from one another, working together at various times on translations of Rumi, Ahmad Shamlou, Nima Yushij, Mehdi Akhavan-Saales, Forough Farrokhzad, and others. When Steve Scholl, at White Cloud Press, asked me if I was interested in creating an expanded edition of *The Green Sea of Heaven: Fifty Ghazals from the Diwan of Háfiz-i Shirazi*, Iraj was happy to join me. We decided to start from the ground up, translating thirty new ghazals, revisiting and revising ones contained in the 1995 edition, and updating the notes and bibliography. It has been a challenge and a joy.

We would like to thank Jim Morris, now at Boston College, for introducing us, and to the scholars, artists, poets, family members, composers, singers, and musicians who have worked and performed Háfiz with us since Green Sea's publication in 1995, in private gatherings as well as at places like Harvard University and the Sackler Museum in Washington, D.C. Yes, Afshin Goodarzi and Ralph Martin, especially you!

We would also like to thank our dear friend of long-standing, the virtuoso musician and world-class artist Reza Derakshani, for the dazzling painting of Khusrau and Shirin that graces the cover of this new edition. Early on he performed and recorded many of these ghazals with us, and we feel his presence in these translations.

LIZ GRAY
NEW YORK CITY

PREFACE TO THE 1995 EDITION

Ultimately the translator is responsible for the choices he or she makes, for what is caught and what is missed. While acknowledging that responsibility, I must be clear that these translations reflect learning over many years from many people.

I have been blessed with advice, instruction, and encouragement from an array of extraordinary scholars, translators, and poets working in the field of Classical Persian. In the early 1970s at Harvard University I learned Persian from Wheeler Thackston, first encountered Háfiz under the encouraging eye of Hossein Ziai, and had the opportunity to study under, and travel briefly in North India with, Annemarie Schimmel. Waris Kirmani, at the University of Aligarh, India, and Farhang Jahanpour and Muhammad Qaʾemi at the University of Isfahan, Iran, both helped me work through a number of ghazals. Bruce Lawrence, at Duke University, and Jim Morris, at the Imperial Iranian Academy of Philosophy and the Institute for Ismaʾili Studies in Paris reviewed early drafts and offered encouragement. In 1989 Michael Sells, at Haverford, urged me to return to the manuscript and revise it for publication and offered insightful suggestions. During the past year Iraj Anvar, at New York University, has collaborated with me on revising the poems and notes. The gentle insistence and suggestions of Steve Scholl at White Cloud Press have been invaluable. The views, learning, and experience of these wise folk, and their own personal responses to Háfiz, have informed my own understanding of his work, and thus shaped these translations. I am grateful for their time, their encouragement, their humor, and their well-grounded skepticisms.

I am also grateful to the poet-translators whose advice has proved important. Elizabeth Bishop, by her example as a translator and her powerful insistence that I focus on what Háfiz actually *said*, was helpful in curbing excesses that arose from early enthusiasm combined with a partial understanding of the Persian. Robert Lowell's terse and scathing dismissal of some early drafts was personally devastating and saved me years of work. Robert Fitzgerald's encouragement, and his stubborn insistence on the value of the work, were helpful when I was working with him and have sustained me since his death. Listening to him share, at great length, his difficulty with a passage of Virgil was one of the most illuminating experiences I have ever had. His long, tangible, complicated, and intimate relationship with Homer and Virgil, and his attention to scholarship as well as poetry, continue to be a source of inspiration. To some degree, these translations remain an offering to him.

ETG, JR.
NEW YORK CITY

NOTE ON TRANSLITERATION

The Persian language is written using the Arabic alphabet. In 1995, we chose a transliteration system that hewed closely to scholarly practice and Library of Congress guidelines, that track orthography rather than pronunciation. The most obvious relic of that choice is our transliteration of the poet's name as *Háfiz* rather than *Háfez*, the latter aligned with how the Persian is actually pronounced. Our decision to retain the original transliterated spelling is driven by our desire not to unravel the thread laid down by the book in search engines and filing systems. It is, after all, the 30th anniversary of the (augmented and revised) original book, not a new book.

TRANSLATORS' INTRODUCTION

Khwája Shams ud-Dín Muhammad Háfiz-i Shírází (d. 1389) is acknowledged to be the unrivalled master of the classical Persian ghazal, a brief and strict lyric form. Throughout the Persian-speaking world one hears his verses recited or sung in the bazaar, on the radio, and at spiritual gatherings. His *Díwán*, or collected works, is held in such high esteem that, like the Qur'án, it is used for divination and augury. Nevertheless, about Háfiz's life we have legends but few facts. We do not even have an authentic text of his *Díwán*.

HÁFIZ AND HIS HISTORICAL CONTEXT

The extant sources of biographical information—a preface to an early edition of his work, anecdotes and biographical sketches, references by other writers, the poems themselves—strengthen some of the legends and bring others into question but are not ultimately reliable. What we have are facts about his life that seem consistent among the sources, and we know that the era in which he lived was one of both political chaos and extraordinary literary and artistic achievement. We know that he lived in one of the most beautiful cities in the world.

Háfiz was born in Isfahan, in what is now central Iran, somewhere between 1317 and 1325. His father, Bahá ud-Dín, was a merchant, and moved his family south from Isfahan to the city of Shiraz when Háfiz was a young boy.[1] Shiraz lies along the banks of the Ruknabad River, in the

---

[1] Sources differ on the date of his birth. Some also say that it was Háfiz's grandfather, rather than his father, who moved to Shiraz from Isfahan. Some give his father's name as Kamal ul-Din. Edward G. Browne's *A Literary History Persia*, volume 3, (1920,

province of Fars, nestled in a circle of mountains and surrounded by vineyards. In Háfiz's day it was a flourishing center of Islamic civilization, and he developed a deep and lifelong affection for the city. Then, as now, it was famous for its beauty, its wines, and its exquisite gardens.

Háfiz's father died when Háfiz was still a child, leaving the family in difficult circumstances. Nevertheless, Háfiz seems to have acquired a thorough and comprehensive classical education. He was fluent in the Persian and Arabic languages and traditions, and educated in the Quranic sciences. His pen name, Háfiz ("the preserver," "the guardian"), implies that he could recite the entire Qur'án from memory, although it can also suggest a singer or musician.[2] He is said to have worked as a baker's apprentice and a copyist until he found adequate patronage for his poetry, and is said to have taught in one of Shiraz's theological schools later in his life.

Háfiz was born in the last days of the Íl-Khánid empire established by Hülegü Khán. A grandson of Chingiz Khán, Hülegü was best known for his sack of Baghdad, the capital of the far reaching 'Abbasid empire, in 1258. During Háfiz's childhood and adolescence the Íl-Khánid empire disintegrated into small rival states and factions. Rebellion, civil war, and intradynastic treachery were common, and cities changed hands many times. A brief discussion of the squabbling dynasties that existed in southern Iran during Háfiz's lifetime will give the modern reader a sense for the context in which Háfiz wrote, and perhaps a better understanding of the poet and his work. Although of little importance in the grand scheme of Islamic history, these minor rulers were the patrons upon whose favor Háfiz depended for his life and livelihood.

While Háfiz was in his teens, Sháh Abú Isháq of the Injú dynasty consolidated power in Fars after a seven-year struggle with his three brothers. Abú Isháq was a tolerant ruler, easy-going and artistically inclined, and brought stability to the region. We know that Háfiz's literary career began to flourish during Abú Isháq's twelve-year reign because several of his poems mention patrons who served as viziers at Abú Isháq's court.[3] In 1353, Abú Isháq was overthrown and eventually executed by Sháh Mubariz ud-Dín Muhammad, founder of the Muzaffarid dynasty based

---

1969) gives an extensive and colorful history of both Háfiz's life and the chaotic times in which he lived.
[2] Nategh, Homa. *Khonyagarí, Mey va Shádí Háfiz-i Shirazi* (2004).
[3] See, for example, Ghazal 9 and related notes.

in Yazd.⁴ In contrast to Abú Isháq, Mubariz embraced a strictly orthodox Islam, and both courtly delights and the taverns of Shiraz suffered during the five years of his puritanical rule.

Despite the artistic chill, and perhaps demonstrating a high degree of skill in political adaptation, Háfiz continued to write at court, perhaps under the patronage of Mubariz's Chief Minister.⁵ Returning from a successful campaign against Isfahan and Tabriz in 1358, Mubariz was deposed, blinded, and thrown in prison by his two sons, who divided their father's kingdom between them. Qutb ud-Dín Mahmud claimed Isfahan, and Jalal ud-Din Shah Shujá began his long reign in Shiraz, which, although troubled, saw the expansion of Shah Shujá's dominion over much of the old Íl-Khánid empire.

Sháh Shujá was not only a consistent patron of the arts and learning, but a poet in his own right, both in Persian and Arabic. It was during his twenty-seven-year reign that Háfiz flourished and wrote the poetry that became famous throughout the Islamic world. Apparently, the relationship between Háfiz and his ruler/patron was not always smooth. One story suggests that Háfiz fell out of favor for mocking both Sháh Shujá's panegyrist,⁶ and those less skilled in crafting of verse (presumably including Sháh Shujá himself). During this time, he is said to have spent one or two years in Isfahan and Yazd, but we have no certain evidence of this. Aside from this interlude of disfavor, and despite lucrative offers of patronage from courts as far away as Baghdad and India, Háfiz could never bring himself to leave Shiraz.

By 1380, when Háfiz was in his sixties, Timur Lang (known to Occidentals as "Tamerlane") had consolidated power in Central Asia north of the Oxus River, and turned his attention to the territories of the old Íl-Khánid empire. In 1380, his assaults on the provinces of Khurasan, Sistan, and Mazandaran laid waste to the countryside and razed any town that tried to defend itself. As an instrument of war his use of terror was meticulous and persuasive: the story of 2,000 defenders of a town in Sistan who were built into a wall while still alive traveled quickly and served as vivid reminder of the price of resistance. In 1382, Timur again came south into Persia, but a negotiated truce between Timur and Sháh Shujá

---

⁴ See notes to Ghazals 9 and 56.
⁵ Supposedly Burhán ud-Dín Faqíh.
⁶ Imád ud-Dín Faqíh was Sháh Shujá's official panegyrist.

ensured that the Muzaffarid possessions were spared the horrors visited upon neighboring provinces.

In 1387, the Muzaffarids were not so lucky. Sháh Shujá had been succeeded by his son Zayn ul-Abidín, who declined to offer obeisance to Timur in person. Aggravated by this display of disrespect Timur marched against Fars, and upon arriving in Isfahan demanded a hefty financial contribution from its inhabitants. The rebuke tendered by the Isfahanis included the killing of several of Timur's tax collectors. In response Timur looted the city and massacred its entire population. He had a tall minaret of 70,000 skulls built as a grim memorial and proceeded south toward Shiraz. Zayn ul-'Abidín fled to Shustar, where he was promptly blinded and imprisoned by his cousin. Timur entered Shiraz without bloodshed.

The legendary meeting between Timur and Háfiz is said to have taken place during Timur's sojourn in Shiraz. Timur is said to have called Háfiz into his presence to scold him for the following *bayt*:

> If that Turk of Shiraz makes me happy, I would give for his Hindu [i.e. black] mole both Bukhara and Samarqand.

Timur pointed out that he had conquered and plundered much of the world in order to build and beautify Bukhara and Samarqand, his native cities and seat of government. He was incensed that Háfiz could suggest trading both for the affection of a young, lithe, Turkish slave with a beauty mark. Háfiz, with a deep bow, is said to have replied, "Sir, it is because such prodigality that I have fallen into poverty and hard times." Timur was apparently charmed, and ordered that Háfiz be rewarded instead of imprisoned.

Between 1387 and 1392 various Muzaffarid brothers and cousins fought for control of Shiraz, Yazd, Kirman, and other cities in Fars. In 1392, Timur ended the family dispute by taking Shiraz and executing the remaining dynastic contenders, with the exception of the blind Zayn ul-'Abidín, whom he took to Samarqand. Timur's pursuit of conquest and terror continued (he executed 100,000 people in Delhi in 1398). Upon his death in 1405 he was succeeded by his son, Sháh Rukh, who had difficulty holding together the empire his father had created.

Háfiz did not live to see the demise of the Muzaffarids. He died in 1389 or 1390, and was buried in the Musalla Gardens, which lie gracefully along the banks of the Ruknabad river in the city he loved so well. As he predicted in several of his ghazals, his tomb and its surrounding gardens became a place of pilgrimage, and remain so to this day.

LITERATURE AT COURT

To understand the role of the poet at court in the fourteenth century we must examine courtly tradition in Persia.[7] Pre-Islamic Persia was primarily an urban society governed by kings who kept their ceremonial distance from the populace and were considered almost, if not actually, divine. Court life was elaborate and elegant, and the formal ranks of the nobility placed great emphasis on courtly manners and appropriate behavior. The king's retinue included musicians, dancers, singers and other entertainers. Of these, the poet's place was considered highly prestigious. Poets and their patrons had a special relationship with one another: the patron provided security, support, and privilege; the poet served as entertainer, panegyrist, and as appropriate, intimate counsellor. Most of this courtly tradition was incorporated by Islamic and Arab rulers, and did not change dramatically during the Mongol era.

In the fourteenth century rulers and their ministers were the primary patrons of the arts, including poetry, and the arts flourished during these turbulent times. Poetry was composed for the patron and his retinue, who were usually well-educated in the Persian and Arabic language and literary traditions. Poetry was recited orally, or sung, in this very public context, as entertainment or diversion, as an offering for a specific occasion, as an entry in a poetic competition, or as a general or specific statement on a topic. Poets used a variety of poetic forms, of which the ghazal was one.

THE GHAZAL

FORMAL REQUIREMENTS

Háfiz's *Díwán* consist almost entirely of ghazals, and he so perfected this formidable verse form that none of his many successors have ever

---

[7] Dominic Brookshaw's *Hafiz and His Contemporaries: Poetry, Performance and Patronage in Fourteenth-Century Iran* (2019) offers a recent and comprehensive overview of Háfiz and the context in which his work was written and performed. Julie Scott Meisami's *Medieval Persian Court Poetry* (1986) discusses at length courtly traditions, the relationship between poet and patron, and the various types of poetry that flourished in that milieu (panegyric odes, romances, and ghazals).

matched his depth, elegance, and precision. The classical Persian ghazal has between five and twelve lines (*bayts*), each of which is divided into two hemistiches (*misra'*). In the opening *bayt*, the *matla'*, each *misra'* ends in an identical rhyme, and this monorhyme is repeated at the end of each *bayt* for the remainder of the poem. Often the rhyme incorporates one or more repeated words (*radíf*), not only the final syllable.

Although Persian is an accentual, Indo-European language, the meters used in Persian verse are quantitative, and were adopted from classical Arabic prosody. The first *misra'* sets the meter to which all other *misra'* conform, although on occasion the poet may substitute two short syllables for one long syllable. Depending on the meter, a *bayt* may have between twenty-four and thirty-two syllables. The rhythmical pattern and rhyme scheme can be seen in the following diagram of a ghazal in a typical meter (*Ramal sálim makhbún mahdhúf*). While the diagram below should be read from left to right, the reader needs to bear in mind that Persian is read from right to left.

```
-o-- oo-- oo-- -- A          -o-- oo-- oo-- -- A
-o-- oo-- oo-- -- B          -o-- oo-- oo-- -- A
-o-- oo-- oo-- -- C          -o-- oo-- oo-- -- A
-o-- oo-- oo-- -- D          -o-- oo-- oo-- -- A
-o-- oo-- oo-- -- E          -o-- oo-- oo-- -- A
-o-- oo-- oo-- -- F          -o-- oo-- oo-- -- A
                 -o-- oo-- oo-- -- G
                 -o-- oo-- oo-- -- A
```

As a rule, the last *bayt* (*maqta'*) contains the poet's name or pen name (*takhallus*). While the complex and rigid requirements of the ghazal form defeated many less talented poets, it forced others, like Háfiz, to write verse of compressed and brilliant intensity.

ORIGINS AND EVOLUTION

While the term ghazal can be used in a general way to mean a genre of lyric poetry concerned primarily with love, in its more restricted sense it means the formal, classical Persian lyric perfected in the thirteenth and fourteenth centuries. From uncertain origins, it has evolved differently in the Arabic, Persian, Ottoman, and Urdu literary traditions.[8]

Some believe that the classical Persian ghazal evolved from the *nasíb*, the brief and often erotic prologue to the Arabic *qasída*, a longer ode with a ghazal-like rhyme scheme composed on panegyric didactic, elegiac, or religious subjects.[9] Others believe the ghazal developed from early Iranian folk poetry, about which we know nothing. Others believe it to be a blending of indigenous Persian lyric with the more formal structures and themes of earlier Arabic poetry.

By the tenth century the traditional themes explored by early ghazal composers had hardened into literary convention. Thereafter, in addition to the rhetorical figures and embellishments required of all good Persian poetry, the conservative taste of the Persian courts demanded that poets continue to improvise on the themes of love, longing, wine, intoxication, separation and sorrow, roses, nightingales, deserts, and departing caravans. Excellence lay not in creating a new or unique image, but in using the familiar images and conventions in innovative ways.

In the twelfth and thirteenth centuries the ghazal underwent a decisive alteration. What had been a courtly love lyric concerned with actual wine and physical beauty became, in the hands of great Sufi writers like Farid ud-Dín 'Attar (1142-1220) and Jalal ud-Dín Rumi (1207-1273), both a vehicle to describe the mystic's loving relationship with God and also a means of veiling from theological and political conservatives the Sufi belief in the possibility of an intuitive, personal union between human beings and God. The infusion of mysticism enriched the ghazal and opened the traditional themes to new dimensions of interpretation. The symbols brought to the form by Sufi writers became, in their turn, literary conventions.

The ghazal reached its high level of formal development with the work of Muslih ud-Dín Sa'adí (1256-1292), also of Shiraz, author of the famous *Gulistán*. His ghazals were beautifully composed around a single theme, usually of a more moralistic than spiritual nature. Fifty years later Háfiz

---

[8] Alessandro Bausani's article on "The Ghazal" and its evolution can be found in the *Encyclopedia of Islam* (Second Edition), and readers seeking more extensive information are advised to begin with this source. In the past few decades the form, with varying degrees of rigor, has been incorporated into English and other poetries.

[9] Jan Rypka. *History of Iranian Literature* (1968). For a thorough introduction to, and translations of, the Arabic *qasída*, see Michael Sell's *Desert Tracings* (1989).

in command of the ghazal's traditional imagery and themes and at home with its intricate formal requirements, blended eroticism, mysticism, and panegyric into verse of unsurpassed beauty.

CONVENTIONS

These ghazals are often puzzling to the westerner who approaches them for the first time. The same images reappear in poem after poem after poem. The poems do not seem to go anywhere: there is no opening, no action, no ultimate resolution or answer. Sometimes the lines seem unrelated to one another. And everything seems ambiguous: is the poet talking to the one he loves? Or is he reproaching a patron? Or is this a nugget of wisdom aimed at the disciple who seeks union with God? If the poet is talking to or about his beloved, is the beloved a man or a woman? Is it actually the poet talking? And isn't drinking alcohol a violation of Islamic law?

At first glance, and in comparison with other classical Persian literary forms—such as the panegyric, the *qasída*, the romance, the narrative *mathnawí*, the witty *rubá'í*—the ghazal seems to be a personal or even confessional poem. The poet seems to share his personal feelings. With time it becomes clear that this is not the case. The poet is using an array of personae and images to speak of love in a way that expresses an ideal, and does so within a fiction. The troubadour poets in medieval Europe crafted their songs in a similar way.

The poet who declares his identity in the closing *bayt* of the ghazal, the voice speaking throughout the ghazal, is a persona. It is the "I" of an "I-Thou" relationship, and the "I" speaks of his searing love for the perpetually unreachable "Thou." The "I" and "Thou" may be lover and beloved, poet and patron, mystic and God, or the poet may intend a *bayt* or ghazal to suggest all of these relationships. However it is framed, the ghazal deals with unconditional love and devotion, the anguish of separation and longing, the ecstasy of union, the creation of obligations, and the honoring of promises.

The ambiguities that surround the speaker and the object of his love stem from a variety of sources. The politics of court and Islamic prohibition against extramarital relationships forced the poet to veil the identity of his beloved. Refined tact and diplomacy were important in addressing powerful and perhaps capricious patrons whose power over one's life and livelihood was absolute. References to things considered heretical by Islam could not be discussed too explicitly.

In addition, poets took advantage of the fact that Persian pronouns do not indicate gender. It is usually impossible to tell whether the beloved is male or female, royal, or divine. Háfiz exploited these ambiguities, powerfully and artfully, to suggest different types of "I- Thou" relationships and to create resonances between them.[10] It is why "every listener seems to find in it an answer to his question, every reader thinks he is discovering an allusion to his desire."[11]

IMAGERY

Háfiz could draw upon, and was constrained by, the rich array of images and analogies that had been used and developed in preceding centuries. To the well-educated courtly listener each image held, embedded within it, a host of associations and recollections. Delighting an audience demanded that the verse act like a prism, bringing different light from new angles to a rich and familiar image. Háfiz used imagery from many sources: stories and sayings from the Islamic tradition, from pre-Islamic Persian epics, Sufi literature, astronomy, astrology, alchemy, geography, commerce, and the flora and fauna of Shiraz's gardens. To offer here a lengthy explanation and analysis of the various elements that make up the ghazals canon of imagery would not be fruitful. Some are discussed in Daryush Shayegan's afterword, others in the footnotes to the individual ghazals.[12] Nevertheless, a brief sketch of the cast of characters and primary images will be helpful to the reader encountering these poems for the first time.

---

[10] While the Persian language's pronouns' ambiguity of gender (and its lack of distinction between upper and lower case letters) enhances the allusiveness available to the poet, the English translator is forced on some occasions to choose between the masculine, the feminine, and the Divine. Throughout these translations we have elected to use lowercase letters unless it is clear that Háfiz is referring to God, and have tried diligently to avoid having to make a choice of gender. Nevertheless, some of our translated ghazals speak of a masculine beloved (a standard assumption in classical Persian poetry), and some of a feminine beloved (a standard assumption in English poetry). Within ghazals we have tried to remain consistent unless a shift seemed appropriate. The reader should continually remember that the original Persian is not so constrained.

[11] See Shayegan, p. 168.

[12] For comprehensive descriptions and analyses of imagery within the Persian poetic tradition in English see Annemarie Schimmel's *A Two-Colored Brocade* (1992) which draws on examples from a range of Islamic literatures, and Dominic Brookshaw's *Hafiz and His Contemporaries* (2019).

There is the beloved, who has the tall and swaying stature of the cypress, a lush snare of dark curls on his/her head, and the radiant, pure, and perfect face of the moon. The lover seeks union with the beloved, to give up his soul to the beloved, to become lost or annihilated in the beloved as the moth is consumed by the flame to which it is attracted. The beloved is the source and incarnation of love and beauty, the ultimately beautiful rose unfolding in the garden, and the lover, pining in separation or loss, begs the dawn wind or the hoopoe to act as a messenger or go-between, to bring him news of the beloved, to carry a message or plaint to him (or her).

The true lover understands the ecstasy and the pain of loving, for him it is both his elixir and daily bread. He is the one for whom love is the sole spiritual imperative, the ultimate intoxicant, the only law that governs an enlightened soul. Lovers are the disciples of beauty, disciples of the beloved, and the disciples of love. They take up the path of love and pass through its waystations under the guidance of a Master, a wise elder (the *pír*). The *rends*[13] are lovers: they adhere only to love's law, and to the uninitiated their behavior seems dissolute and blasphemous.

Arrayed in opposition to the lover are the false lovers and the enforcers of orthodoxy. The orthodox scholars and judges preach and enforce the Islamic law, or *sharí'a*. They condemn intoxication, demand penitence, and insist on correct behavior. Háfiz mocks them because in their blind adherence to the letter of Islamic law they miss God and His message completely. Their own corrupt behavior is at variance with their preaching and prohibitions. They are blind to what matters.[14]

There is also the *raghíb*, "chaperone" (or "rival" in contemporary Persian) who prevents access to the beloved, and the *mudda'í,* the "impostor" or "pretender," who claims to understand Love, and claims intimacy with the beloved. The imposter's words are empty of wisdom, he is not an intimate of the secrets. Nevertheless, he babbles on about love, offering his audience unenlightened verse.

A word on taverns, wine, wine masters, cupbearers, and Zoroastrians is in order. Islam's prohibition against drinking alcohol meant that within the Islamic world the making and serving of wine fell to the Zoroastrians and Christians and others. Nevertheless, in Háfiz's ghazals the "tavern of

---

[13] See Shayegan, p. 180 et ff.
[14] See, for example, Háfiz's subversive audacity, his continuing role as "one of the greatest protesters in history," Shayegan, p. 183.

the Magi" usually suggests an esoteric sanctuary or gathering, and assembly of believers, which exists beyond the borders of orthodox Islam. It was wise to veil one's speech when discussing such things.

Wine drinking parties were a regular and elaborate fixture of courtly life.[15] At these gatherings wine was served by young Turkic slaves, imported from northern Iran and central Asia as children. They were taught weaponry and riding, to sing and to serve wine. They were thought most beautiful just at the moment they entered puberty, when the first traces of facial hair became visible. These cupbearers were the object of poetic and physical love. While in western literature we are unaccustomed to, and often uncomfortable with, homoerotic love, the reader should understand that by convention the beloved is male.

UNITY: AN ONGOING DEBATE

To the reader accustomed to western literature, a first encounter with a ghazal is puzzling and perhaps frustrating: there is no plot, no narrative, no movement toward a climax or resolution in the way that westerners understand dramatic development. Indeed, depending on the edition, the *bayts* in a specific ghazal may appear in different sequences, rarely affecting the ghazal's power as a poem.

Apparently Sháh Shujá' was the first person to raise the question of whether, or in what manner, there is unity in Háfiz's ghazals. Háfiz supposedly answered to the effect that most people seemed to like his poems, and that in fact while other poets had trouble finding an audience beyond their own city gates, Háfiz's poems were read throughout the Islamic world.[16] While acknowledging the truth of Háfiz's response, others continue to debate Sháh Shujá's question. Opinions as to whether the ghazals have unity, and if so, in what way, and does it matter, have varied with the fashions of literary criticism.[17]

Some western critics decided that atomism was the defining principle:

---

[15] See Brookshaw, *Hafiz and His Contemporaries*, and "The Theme of Wine Drinking and the Concept of the Beloved in Early Persian Poetry," by Ehsan Yarshater, 1960.
[16] Michael Hillman, *Unity in the Ghazals of Háfiz* (1976), p. 8, 47.
[17] Some of the primary contributors to this discussion have been Arberry, Rehder, Wickens, Hillman, Boyce, Meisami, Schimmel, and Brookshaw. The reader who wishes to explore this topic further, or to see how differing theories are applied to specific ghazals, should begin with these authors.

there was no unifying element, each *bayt* was like a perfect, separate pearl. The ghazal was simply a series of pearls on a string of a certain length, "orient pearls at random strung."[18] Other readers have felt a sense of completeness, of "unity," in a Háfizean ghazal, and have tried in different ways to describe its source. Some find it to be similar to the pattern in a carpet or tapestry: variations of shape and color that repeat and connect to form a whole. Others describe it as a crystal, each facet illuminating a different aspect of one or several themes. Some have described the ghazal as polyphonic or contrapuntal, having two or three themes that weave together, and recur in different forms, in different registers. Some have likened the ghazal to the surface of a pool: from two or three themes dropped like pebbles or resonance. Suffice it to say that, although the form has become popular with contemporary poets, ghazals are not like any western lyric. For centuries people have been deeply moved by these poems, and I would urge the reader approaching ghazals for the first time to question their own embedded literary assumptions and to brandish lightly, at the outset, the templates of western literary criticism.

TEXTUAL PROBLEMS

We have no established text of Háfiz's *Díwán* and it seems that Háfiz did not compile one during his lifetime.[19] The editions that proliferated throughout the Islamic world after his death attest to the quality and fame of his work, but as they grew in number the texts themselves became more corrupt. Even if Háfiz had circulated different versions of specific ghazals, or had revised and edited earlier ghazals as he went along, it would not explain the alterations and expanded editions. Copyists the world over are likely to misread or miscopy manuscripts and might "improve" a *bayt* by substituting a "better" word, but it seems that lines in similar meters by other authors, or whole ghazals, may have been added to "enhance" the edition. Lesser writers may have sought to ensure that their work would live forever by inserting a ghazal of their own among those of Háfiz.

Since the early sixteenth century efforts have been made to define

---

[18] Sir William Jones, "A Persian Song," 1771, in A. J. Arberry's, "Háfiz and His English Translators" (1946).
[19] Rehder's "The Text of Háfiz" (1974) and "New Material for the Text of Háfiz" (1967) offer a comprehensive discussion of the *Díwán*'s history, and the existing textual problems.

an authentic *Díwán*. The preface to an early edition by Háfiz's "friend" Gulandam suggests that it is a first edition, but that assumption has not been tested. Qazvíní's and Ghání's 1941 critical edition was based on the oldest manuscripts available at the time, and in their judgment none of the four manuscripts upon which they relied was related to the others. Since 1941 at least fourteen manuscripts have come to light that appear to pre-date the ones used by Qazvíní and Ghání, but they have not been extensively studied in relation to one another. More work needs to be done, and may or may not result in an authentic text.

Khánlari's edition was used for these translations and the editions by Qazvíní and Ghání, by Ahmad and Ná'íní, and by Anjaví were consulted. In addition, we have drawn extensively on the commentaries by Khorramsháhi, Rajá'í, Súdí, and Bargnaysi, and consulted teachers, scholars, and advisors in the U.S., Iran, and India, as well as previous translations of Háfiz's work.

THE GHAZALS

یک

الا یـا اَیُـها السّـاقی اَدِر کَأسَاً وَ نـاوِلها
که عِشـق آسـان نِمود اوّل وَلی اُفتـاد مُشکِلهـا

بـه بـویِ نـافِـه‌یی کـاخِر صَبـا زان طُرّه بگشـاید
زِ تـابِ جَعدِ مشکینش چه خون افتاد در دلهـا

بـه مِـی سَجّادِه رَنگین کُن گَرت پیر مُغان گوید
که سـالِک بـی خَبر نَبوَد زِ راه و رسـمِ مَنزِلهـا

مـرا در منزِلِ جـانان چه اَمنِ عَیش چونِ هَردَم
جَرَس فـریاد می‌دارَد که بَربَندید مَحمِلهـا

شبِ تـاریک و بیـم مَوج و گِردابی چُنین هـایل
کجـا دانند حـالِ مـا سَبُکبـاران سـاحِلهـا

هَمِه کـارَم زِ خودکامی بـه بَدنامی کَشید آخِر
نَهان کِی مـانَد آن رازی کَزان سـازَند مَحفِلهـا

حُضـوری گر هَمـی خواهـی ازو غـایِب مشو حافظ
مَتـی مـا تَلـقَ مَن تَهـوی دَعِ الدُّنیـا وَ اَهمِلهـا

ONE

O *saqi!* bring around the cup of wine and offer it to me,
for love seemed easy at first but then grew difficult.

Those who wait for the scent that the dawn wind may spill
from those dark musky curls—how terribly they suffer.

Stain your prayer mat with wine if the Magus tells you to,
for such a traveler knows the road and the customs of its stations.

What security is there for me here in her caravanserai
when every moment the camel bells cry, "Pack up the litters!"

The dark night, the fear of waves, the terrifying whirlpool,
how can they know of our state, those who go lightly along the shore?

In the end, my life has gone from self-absorption to ill-repute.
Where can a secret stay hidden if people gather to discuss it?

Háfiz, if you desire to be in her presence, pay attention.
When you find what you seek, abandon the world and let it go.

دو

صَلاحِ کار کُجا وُ مـنِ خَراب کُجا
بِبین تَفاوتِ رَه کَز کُجاست تا بِه کُجا

چِه نِسبَت است بِه رِندی صَلاح و تقوا را
سَماعِ وَعظ کُجا نَغمهٔ رَباب کُجا

دلَم زِ صوِمعِه بِگرِفت و خِرقهٔ سالوس
کُجاست دِیرِ مُغان و شَرابِ ناب کُجا

بِشُد، کِه یادِ خوَشش باد روزگارِ وصال
خود آَن کِرشمه کُجا رفت و آن عِتاب کُجا

زِ رویِ دوسَت دِلِ دُشمَنان چِه دَریابَد
چِراغِ مُــرده کُجا شَمعِ آفتاب کُجا

مَبین بِه سیبِ زَنَخدان کِه چاهِ در راه است
کُجا هَمی رَوی ای دِل بِدین شِتاب کُجا

چو کُحلِ بِینشِ ما خاکِ آستانِ شِماست
کُجا رَویم بِفَرما از این جِنابِ کُجا

قَرار و خَواب زِ حافظ طَمَع مَدار ای دوست
قَرار چیست صَبوری کَدام و خَواب کُجا

TWO

There is the righteous one, here is ruined me.
See how far it is from one to the other!

What link do righteousness and piety have to the rend's way?
There is the sound of preaching, here is the melody of the rebab.

My heart is tired of the cloister and the hypocrite's cloak.
Where is the monastery of the Magi? Where is pure wine?

The days of union are gone. Let them be a joyful memory.
Where is that amorous glance? Where is that reproach?

What can the enemy's heart find in my love's face?
There is that dead lamp. Here is this sun candle.

Don't be distracted by her dimple, for it's an abyss in the road.
Where are you going, O heart, in such a hurry?

Since the kohl of our insight is the dust of your doorway,
please tell us, where do we go from this threshold? Where?

Do not covet rest and sleep from Háfiz, O friend.
What is rest? Which is patience? And where is sleep?

سه

صَبا به لُطف بِگو آن غَزال رَعنا را
که سَر به کوه و بیابان تو دادهای ما را

شِکّر فُروش که عُمرَش دراز باد چرا
تَفَقُّدی نَکُنَد طوطیِ شِکَرخا را

چو با حَبیب نِشینیّ و بادِه پیمایی
به یاد دار مُحِبّانِ بادپیما را

غرورِ حُسن اِجازَت مَگر نداد ای گُل
که پُرسِشی نَکُنی عَندَلیب شِیدا را

به خُلق و لُطف توان کرد صیدِ أَهل نَظَر
به دام و دانه نَگیرَند مُرغِ دانا را

ندانَم از چه سَبَب رَنگِ آشنایی نیست
سَهی قَدانِ سیَه چَشمِ ماه سیما را

جُزین قَدَر نَتَوان گفت در جَمالِ تو عیب
که وَضعِ مِهر و وَفا نیست رویِ زیبا را

در آسمان نه عَجَب گر به گفتهٔ حافظ
سُرودِ زُهره به رَقص آوَرَد مَسیحا را

THREE

O dawn wind, gently say to that graceful gazelle:
"We wander the mountains and desert because of you."

Long life to the sugar-seller! But why doesn't he ask
after the sweet-toothed parrot?

When you sit with the beloved and measure out wine
remember the lovers who measure and drink only wind.

Perhaps your proud beauty keeps you, O rose,
from asking after the frenzied nightingale?

With good nature and kindness you can stalk the insightful ones.
The bird of wisdom can't be caught with rope or snare.

I don't know why the tall, dark-eyed, moon-faced ones
bear no trace of friendliness.

One can speak of no fault in your beauty except for this:
there is no affection or loyalty in a lovely face.

In the heavens it's no wonder that when Venus sings Háfiz's verse
even the Messiah starts to dance.

چهار

صوفی بیا که آینهٔ صافیست جام را
تا بنگری صفای می لعل فام را

راز درون پرده ز رندان مست پرس
کاین حال نیست زاهد عالی مقام را

عنقا شکار کس نشود دام باز چین
کان جا همیشه باد به دست است دام را

در عیش نقد کوش که چون آبخور نماند
آدم بهشت روضهٔ دارُالسّلام را

در بزم دور یک دو قدح درکش و برو
یعنی طمع مدار وصال دوام را

ای دل شباب رفت و نچیدی گلی ز عیش
پیرانه سر بکن هنری ننگ و نام را

ما را بر آستان تو بس حقّ خدمت است
ای خواجه بازبین به ترحّم غلام را

حافظ مرید جام می است ای صبا برو
وز بنده بندگی برسان شیخ جام را

FOUR

Sufi, the mirror of the cup is clear. Come
and see the purity of this ruby wine.

Ask the drunken rends about the veiled secret
for this state is not for the "highly-ranked" ascetic.

The 'anqá is no one's prey. Pick up your snare:
there is nothing to catch but wind.

In life, be content with what you have.
Because of his discontent Adam lost the garden.

This world and the wine go round. At this banquet
drain a cup or two and go—that is, don't be greedy for more of this.

O heart, youth has gone, and you didn't pick life's rose.
In old age make something useful of your reputation.

We who serve you have a claim, here, on your threshold.
O lord, look again, with compassion, on your slave.

Háfiz is the disciple of the wine cup. O dawn wind, go,
and take my devotion to the Shaikh of Jám.

پنج

رَونَقِ عَهدِ شَباب است دِگَر بُستان را
مـی‌رسد مُـژدهٔ گُل بُلبُلِ خـوش اَلحـان را

ای صبـا گَر بِه جوانانِ چَمَن بـازرَسـی
خِـدمَتِ مـا بِرسان سَرو و گُل و رِیحـان را

گَر چُنین جِلوِه کُنَد مُغ بَچهٔ بادِه فُروش
خـاکروبِ درِ مِیخانِه کُـنَم مُـژگان را

ای که بر مَه کِشـی از عَنبَر سارا چَوگان
مُضطَرِب حال مَگَردان مَنِ سَرگَردان را

تَرسَم آن قَوم کـه بر دُردکِشـان می‌خندند
در سَرِ کارِ خَـرابات کُنَند اِیمـان را

یارِ مردانِ خدا بـاش که در کَشتـی نـوح
هست خاکی که به آبی نَخَرد طوفان را

هرکه را خوابگه آخِر نَه که مُشتی خاک است
گو چـه حاجَت که بر اَفلاک کِشی اِیوان را

بُرو از خانـهٔ گردون به دَر و نـان مَطلَب
کان سیَه کاسِه درآخِر بِکُشَد مِهمان را

مـاهِ کَنعـانیِ مـن مَسنَدِ مِصر آن تـو شد
وَقتِ آن است که بِدرود کُنی زِندان را

حافظا مـی خور و رِندی کُن و خوشِ باش وَلی
دَام تَـزویـر مَـکَـن چـون دِگران قرآن را

FIVE

Youth has come again, in its splendor, to the garden.
The sweet-voiced nightingale hears news of the rose.

O dawn wind, if you return to the field of newly-blossomed ones
send my greetings to the rose, the cypress, and the rest.

If the graceful Magian boy reveals himself like this
I will sweep the tavern's doorway with my eyelashes.

You draw your curl of dark hair across your beautiful face.
I am disoriented already. Don't make it worse.

Once inside the tavern I'm afraid that those
who laugh at the dreg-drinkers will lose their faith.

Befriend the people of God, for to the soil in Noah's ark
the flood was just a drop of water.

If our final resting place is but a handful of dust
why do you need to build a palace to the sky?

Leave the house of the world and don't ask it for bread,
for in the end that miser kills its guests.

O Joseph, my moon of Canaan, the throne of Egypt is yours.
It's time for you to say goodbye to this prison.

O Háfiz, be a rend, drink wine, and be happy, but
do not, like others, make the Qur'an a snare of hypocrisy.

شش

ای شـاهِدِ قُدسی کِه کِشَد بند نقابَت
وی مرغِ بِهِشتی کِه دِهَد دانـه و آبَت

خوابَم بِشُد از دیده در این فِکرِ جِگَر سوز
کاغوشِ کِه شُد مَنزِلِ آسایش و خوابَت

دَرویش نمی‌پُرسی و تَرسَم کِه نَبـاشَد
اَنـدیشـهٔ آمُـرزِش و پَـروایِ ثَوابَت

راهِ دلِ عُشـاق زَد آن چَشمِ خُمارین
پیداست از این شیوه که مَست است شَرابَت

تیری که زدی بَر دلَم از غَمزه خَطا رَفت
تا باز چِه اَندیشـه کُنَد رایِ صَوابَت

هـر نـالِه و فَریاد که کَردَم نَشِنیدی
پیداست نِگارا کـه بُلَند است جِنابَت

دور است سَرِ آب از این بادیه هُشدار
تا غولِ بیابان نَفَریبَد به سَرابَت

تا در رَهِ پیری به چِه آیین رَوی ای دل
باری به غَلَط صَرف شد اَیّامِ شَبابَت

ای قَصرِ دِل اَفروز که مَنزِلگَه اُنسی
یـا رَب مَکُنـاد آفَتِ اَیّامِ خَرابَت

جافظ نـه غُلامیست کـه از خواجه گُریزد
لُطفی کُن و بازآ که خَرابَم زِ عِتابَت

SIX

O divine beauty, who will pull aside your veil?
O bird of paradise, who will give you seeds and water?

I burned all night with this thought:
whose arms are your home and sleeping-place?

You never ask after me, the dervish, and I fear that you give
no thought to salvation and good works.

Your drunken eyes stole the lovers' hearts.
This makes it clear that your eyes are drunk.

The arrow of your sultry glance went astray and missed my heart.
Let's see what your righteous judgment will think of next.

I moaned and shouted but you heard nothing.
It's apparent, my beauty, that your doorway is out of reach.

Distant is the spring in this desert. Beware
that the ghoul of the desert doesn't conjure a mirage.

Let's see how well you will fare on the road of old age, O heart,
given that you spent the days of your youth in error.

O beloved, you who are the dwelling-place of intimacy,
may God preserve you from the ravages of time.

Háfiz is not a slave who runs from his master.
Be kind and come back, for I am a wreck without your reproach.

هفت

مَطلَب طاعَت و پیمان و صَلاح از من مَست
که بـه پیمانه کِشی شُهره شُدَم روزِ اَلَست

من هَمان دَم که وُضو ساختَم از چِشمهٔ عشق
چارتَکبیر زَدَم یِکسَره بَر هَر چه که هَست

مِی بِدِه تا دِهَمَت آگَهی از سِرِّ قَضا
که به رویِ کِه شدَم عاشِق و از بویِ کِه مَست

کَمَرِ کوه کَم است از کَمَرِ مور آنجا
نا امید از دَرِ رَحمَت مَشو ای بادِه پَرَست

بـه جُز آن نَرگسِ مَستانه که چَشمَش مَرساد
زیرِ این طارُمِ فیروزه کَسی خوش نَنِشَست

جان فَدای دَهَنَش باد که در باغ نَظَر
چَمَن آرایِ جَهان خوشتَر از این غُنچه نَبَست

حافظ از دولتِ عشقِ تو سُلیمانی شُد
یعنی از وَصلِ توّاش نیسَت بِه جُز باد بِه دست

SEVEN

Don't look for obedience, fidelity, and righteousness from drunken me.
I've been known as a drunkard since before creation.

The moment I made my ablutions at the spring of love
I finished the last rites for all that exists.

Give me wine so that I can tell you fate's secrets:
whose face made me fall in love, whose scent made me drunk.

There, the mountain's waist is thinner than that of the ant,
so, O wine-lover, don't give up hope for the threshold of grace.

Aside from that intoxicating narcissus (may it escape the evil eye)
no one has sat happily under this turquoise dome.

May my soul be a sacrifice to your lips, for in the garden of vision
the Gardener of the World has never grown a more beautiful bud.

From the bounty of your love Háfiz became a Solomon.
That is, union with you means he holds only wind in his hand.

هشت

چو بِشنَوی سُخَنِ اَهلِ دِل مَگو که خَطاست
سُخَن شِناس نِئی دِلبرا خَطا این جاست

سَرَم به دُنیی و عُقبی فُرو نمی‌آید
تَبارَکَالله ازین فِتنه‌ها که در سَرِ ماست

در اَندرونِ منِ خَسته دِل نَدانَم کیست
که مَن خَموشَم و او در فَغان و در غَوغاست

دِلَم زِ پَرده بُرون شُد کُجایی ای مُطرب
بِنال هـان که از این پَرده کارِ ما به نَواست

مَرا به کارِ جَهان هَرگِز التِفات نَبود
رُخِ تو در نَظَرِ من چُنین خوشَش آراست

نَخُفته‌ام زِ خیالی که می‌پَزَم شب‌هاست
خُمارِ صَد شَبه دارَم شَرابخانه کُجاست

چُنین که صَومِعه آلوده شُد زِ خونِ دِلَم
گَرَم به بادَه بِشویید حَق به دَستِ شُماست

از آن به دیرِ مُغانَم عَزیز می‌دارَند
که آتشی که نَمیرَد هَمیشه در دِلِ ماست

چه ساز بود که در پَرده می‌زَد آن مُطرب
که رَفت عُمر و دَماغَم هنوز پُر زِ هَواست

نِدای عِشقِ تو دوشَم دَر اَندَرون دادَند
فَضای سینهٔ حافِظ هَنوز پُر زِ صِداست

EIGHT

When you hear the words of those who know, don't say they are wrong.
You do not understand such speech, my lovely one. That is what's wrong.

I do not acknowledge this world or the next.
God be praised for these heretical thoughts.

I don't know who is within wounded-hearted me
that I am silent while he shouts and moans.

My heart has dropped its veil. Where are you, O minstrel?
Sing your songs that will save me.

I never cared about worldly things. To my eyes
your face gave them their beauty.

The thoughts churning in my head keep me awake.
I've had a hangover for months. Where is the tavern?

Given how my heart's blood stained the cloister,
you have the righteous authority to wash me with wine.

They cherish me in the Zoroastrian temple
because the flame in my heart never dies.

What melody did the minstrel play behind the veil
that life has gone by and my mind is still filled with joy?

Last night your love echoed within me.
The inside of Háfiz's heart is still filled with that sound.

۹

ساقی به نورِ باده بَر اَفروز جامِ ما
مُطرِب بگو که کارِ جَهان شُد به کامِ ما

ما در پیاله عَکسِ رُخِ یار دیدهایم
ای بی خَبَر زِ لَذَّتِ شُربِ مُدامِ ما

چَندان بُوَد کِرِشمِه وُ نازِ سَهی قَدان
کاید به جِلوِه سَروِ صِنوبَر خَرامِ ما

هَرگِز نَمیرَد آن که دِلَش زِنده شُد به عشق
ثَبت است بَر جَریدهٔ عالَم دَوامِ ما

تَرسَم که صَرفِه‌ای نَبَرد روزِ بازخواست
نانِ حَلالِ شِیخ زِ آبِ حَرامِ ما

مَستی به چَشمِ شاهِدِ دِلبَندِ ما خوش است
زان رو سپُردهاَند به مَستی زَمامِ ما

ای باد اَگر به گُلشَنِ اَحباب بُگذَری
زِنهار عَرضِه دِه بَرِ جانان پَیامِ ما

گو نامِ ما زِ یاد به عَمدا چِه می‌بَری
خود آیَد آن که یاد نیاری زِ نامِ ما

حافظ زِ دیده دانهٔ اَشکی هَمی فِشان
باشَد که مُرغِ وَصل کُنَد قَصدِ دامِ ما

دریای اَخضَرِ فَلَک و کَشتیِ هِلال
هستند غَرقِ نِعمَتِ حاجیِ قَوامِ ما

NINE

Saqi! Make our cup blaze with winelight!
Sing, minstrel, the world has become as we wished!

O you who don't understand our joy in perpetual drinking,
in our cup we have seen the image of his face.

There are the winks and flirtations of the slender ones only until
our graceful cypress-pine sways into view.

He whose heart has been revived by love will never die.
In the ledger of the world we are marked "Eternal."

I fear that on Resurrection Day the shaikh's holy bread
will be worth no more than our damned wine.

To the eye of my beloved drunkenness is good,
so they have entrusted our reins to drunkenness.

O wind, if you should pass through the garden of the friends,
be sure to give them my message,

say, "Why do you try so hard to forget my name?
That time when no one will remember will come on its own."

Háfiz, keep scattering the grain of your tears.
Perhaps the bird of union will fly into our snare.

The green sea of heaven and the hull of the new moon
are both swamped by the generosity of our Hájjí Qavám.

ده

ای نسیم سَحَر آرامگَهِ یار کُجاست
مَنزِلِ آن مَهِ عاشِق کُشِ عَیّار کُجاست

شبِ تار است و رَهِ وادیِ اَیمَن در پیش
آتشِ طور کُجا موعِدِ دیدار کُجاست

هرکه آمد به جَهان نقشِ خَرابی دارد
در خَرابات بگویید که هُشیار کُجاست

آن کَس است اهلِ بِشارَت که اِشارَت دانَد
نُکته‌ها هَست بَسی مَحرَمِ اَسرار کُجاست

هر سَرِ مویِ مَرا با تو هِزاران کار اِست
ما کُجاییم و مَلامَتگَرِ بی‌کار کُجاست

عقل دیوانهِ شُد آن سِلسِلهٔ مشکین کو
دل زِما گوشه گِرِفت اَبرویِ دِلدار کُجاست

ساقی و مُطرب و می جُمله مُهَیّاست ولی
عِیش بی یار مُهَیّا نَشَوَد یار کُجاست

حافظ از بادِ خَزانِ در چَمَنِ دَهر مَرَنج
فِکرِ مَعقول بِفرما گُلِ بی‌خار کُجاست

TEN

O dawn wind, where is my love's resting-place?
Where is the moon's house, that rogue, that killer of lovers?

The night is dark, the road to the valley of safety lies ahead.
Where is the fire on Sinai? Where is the moment of meeting?

Each one who comes into this world bears the mark of ruin.
In the tavern ask, "Where is the sober one?"

He who understands signs lives with glad tidings.
There are many subtleties. Where is an intimate of the secrets?

Every tip of our hair has a thousand ties to you.
Where are we? And where is the accuser idle?

Reason went mad. Where are those musk-scented chains?
Our heart withdrew from us. Where is the arch of her brow?

Wine, minstrel, and rose are all ready but
there is no pleasure in celebrating without her. Where is she?

Háfiz, don't take offense at autumn's wind over the field of the world.
Think rationally: where is the thornless rose?

یازده

خلوت گُزیده را به تَماشا چه حاجَت است
چون کویِ دوست هست به صَحرا چه حاجَت است

جانا به حاجَتی که تو را هَست با خُدای
کاخِر دَمی بپُرس که ما را چه حاجَت است

ای پادشاهِ حُسنِ خُدا را بِسوختیم
آخِر سُؤال کُن که گِدا را چه حاجَت است

اربابِ حاجَتیم و زَبانِ سُؤال نیست
در حَضرَتِ کَریم تَمَنّا چه حاجَت است

مُحتاجِ قِصّه نیست گَرَت قَصدِ خونِ ماست
چون رَخت از آنِ توست به یَغما چه حاجَت است

جامِ جَهان نَماست ضَمیرِ مُنیرِ دوست
اِظهارِ اِحتیاجِ خود آنجا چه حاجَت است

آن شُد که بارِ مِنَّتِ مَلاح بُردَمی
گوهَر چو دَست داد به دَریا چه حاجَت است

ای عاشِقِ گِدا چو لَبِ روح بَخشِ یار
می‌دانَدَت وَظیفه تَقاضا چه حاجَت است

ای مُدَّعی بُرو که مَرا با تو کار نیست
احَبابِ حاضِرَند به اَعدا چه حاجَت است

حافظ تو خَتم کُن که هُنَرِ خود عَیان شَوَد
با مُدَّعی نِزاع و مُحاکا چه حاجَت است

ELEVEN

For the recluse, what need is there of spectacle?
In the friend's alleyway, what need is there of scenery?

O beloved, by the need that you have for God,
at least for a moment, ask what I need.

O king of beauty, by God, I burn.
At least ask, "What does the beggar need?"

We are the lords of need but have no tongue to ask.
In the presence of the Generous One what need is there for pleading?

If you intend to take our soul there is no need for explanation.
Since all we have is yours what need is there to plunder?

The world-revealing cup is my love's luminous heart,
where there is no need to show your need.

I am no longer in debt to the diver.
Since the pearl has come to hand, who needs the sea?

O lovesick beggar, when your love's life-giving lip
knows what you need, what need is there to ask?

Impostor, go, for I have no business with you.
The friends are here, what need is there of foes?

Finish this, Háfiz, to let your talent show.
With the impostor, who needs to argue and debate?

دوازده

بیا که قصرِ اَمَل سَخت سُست بُنیادَست
بیار بادِه که بُنیادِ عُمر بر بادَست

غُلامِ هِمَّت آنَم که زیرِ چَرخِ کَبود
زِ هَر چه رَنگِ تَعَلُّق پَذیرَد آزادَست

چه گویَمَت که به میخانه دوش مَست و خَراب
سُروشِ عالَمِ غیبَم چه مُژده‌ها دادَست

که ای بُلَند نَظَر شاهبازِ سِدره نشین
نَشیمَنِ تو نه این کُنجِ مِحنَت آبادَست

تو را زِ کُنگِرهٔ عَرش می‌زَنَند صَفیر
نَدانَمَت که درین دامگَه چه افتادَست

نَصیحَتی کُنَمَت یاد گیر و در عَمَل آر
که این حَدیث زِ پیرِ طَریقَتَم یادَست

مَجو دُرُستیِ عَهد از جَهانِ سُست نَهاد
که این عَجوز عَروسِ هِزار دامادَست

غَمِ جَهان مَخور و پَندِ من مَبَر از یاد
که این لَطیفهٔ عِشقَم زِ رهروی یادَست

رضا به داده بِدِه وَز جَبین گِره بِگُشای
که بَر مَن و تو درِ اِختیار نَگشادَست

نشانِ عَهد و وَفا نیست در تَبَسُّمِ گُل
بِنال بُلبُلِ بی‌دِل که جای فَریادَست

حَسَد چه می‌بَری ای سُست نَظم بَر حافِظ
قَبولِ خاطِر و لُطفِ سُخَن خُدادادَست

TWELVE

Believe me, the palace of hope has very weak foundations.
Bring wine, for life is built on the wind.

Under this dark blue dome I am the slave of the power
of the one who is untainted by attachment.

How can I tell you of the good news I heard from the invisible world
last night when I sat, drunk and ruined, in the tavern:

"O royal falcon of keen vision, perched in the seat of honor,
your nest is not this corner filled with suffering;

they whistle to recall you to the battlements of heaven.
I don't understand what has ensnared you here."

I give you some advice, learn it, and in practice remember it,
for it comes to me from my master of the way:

"Do not seek an honest vow from the fickle world,
for this crone is the bride of a thousand grooms."

Don't fret about the world and don't forget my advice,
for I recall this maxim of love from a fellow traveler:

"Consent to what has been given, and loosen the knot of your brow,
because the door of free will is closed to you and me."

The rose's smile bears no trace of loyalty or kept promises.
Feel free to cry, lover-nightingale, it's called-for.

O you who write weak verse, why be jealous of Háfiz?
To reach the heart, to craft graceful verse—these are gifts from God.

سیزده

درین زمانه رفیقی که خالی از خلل است
صُراحیِ می ناب و سَفینهٔ غزل است

جَریده رو که گُذرگاهِ عافیَت تنگ است
پیاله گیر که عُمرِ عزیز بی‌بَدَل است

نه من ز بی عَمَلی در جَهان مَلولَم و بَس
مَلالتِ عُلَما هَم ز علمِ بی‌عَمَل است

به چشمِ عقل در این رَهگذارِ پُرآشوب
جَهان و کارِ جَهان بی‌ثُبات و بی‌مَحَل است

دلم اُمیدِ فراوان به وصلِ رویِ تو داشت
ولی اَجَل به رَهِ عُمر رهزنِ اَمَل است

بگیر طُرّهٔ مَه چهره‌ای و قصّه مَخوان
که سَعد و نَحس ز تأثیرِ زُهره و زُحَل است

به هیچ دَور نَخواهَند یافت هُشیارَش
چُنین که حافظِ ما مَستِ بادهٔ اَزَل است

THIRTEEN

In these times the only untainted companions left
are a jug of pure wine and a book of ghazals.

Travel lightly, the pass of salvation is narrow.
Lift a glass, there is no substitute for this dear life.

I'm not the only one in the world afflicted with idleness;
the theologians also don't practice what they preach.

On this turmoil-filled road the eye of reason
knows the world and its works are fleeting and worthless.

My heart longed for union with you
but on life's road death plunders the caravans of hope.

Grasp the curl of a moon-faced one and stop babbling
that good luck and bad are the work of Venus and Saturn.

Our Háfiz is so drunk on the wine of pre-eternity
that in no epoch will you ever find him sober.

چهارده

زُلف آشُفته و خوی کرده و خَندان لَب و مَست
پیرهَن چاک و غَزَل خوان و صُراحی در دَست

نَرگِسَش عَربَده جوی و لَبَش اَفسوس کنان
نیم‌شَب دوش به بالینِ مَن آمَد بِنِشَست

سَر فَرا گوشِ مَن آوَرد و به آوازِ حَزین
گفت ای عاشِقِ دیرینهٔ من خوابَت هَست

عارِفی را که چُنین بادهٔ شَبگیر دِهَند
کافرِ عِشق بُوَد گَر نَبُوَد بادِه پَرَست

برو ای زاهِد و بَر دُردکشان خُرده مَگیر
که نَدادَند جُز این تُحفه به ما روزِ اَلَست

آنچه او ریخت به پیمانهٔ ما نوشیدیم
اگر از خَمرِ بِهِشت است وگر از بادهٔ مَست

خندهٔ جامِ می و زُلفِ گِره گیرِ نگار
ای بَسا تَوبَه که چون تَوبهٔ حافظ بِشِکَست

FOURTEEN

Curls disheveled, sweating, smiling, and drunk,
shirt torn, singing ghazals, jug in hand,

a quarrel in his eyes, mockery on his lips,
last night at midnight he came and sat by my pillow.

He bent his head to my ear and with a sad voice said,
"O my ancient lover, how can you sleep?"

The seeker to whom they give such a cup at dawn
is an infidel to love if he will not worship wine.

O ascetic, go, and don't quibble with the dreg-drinkers,
for on the eve of creation this was the only gift they gave us.

Whatever he poured in our cup, we drank,
whether the mead of heaven or the wine of drunkenness.

The wine-cup's smile and the beloved's knotted curls
have broken many vows of repentance, like that of Háfiz.

پانزده

روضهٔ خُلدِ بَرین خَلوَتِ دَرویشان است
مایهٔ مُحتَشِمی خِدمَتِ دَرویشان است

گَنجِ عُزلَت که طِلِسماتِ عَجایب دارد
فَتحِ آن در نَظَرِ رَحمَتِ دَرویشان است

قَصرِ فِردوس که رِضوانش به دَربانی رَفت
مَنظری از چَمَنِ نزهَتِ دَرویشان است

آنچه زَر می‌شَوَد از پَرتوِ آن قَلبِ سیاه
کیمیایی‌ست که در صُحبَتِ دَرویشان است

آن که پیشَش بِنهَد تاجِ تَکَبُّر خورشید
کِبریایی‌ست که در حِشمَتِ دَرویشان است

دَولَتی را که نَباشد غَم از آسیبِ زَوال
بی‌تَکَلُّف بِشِنو دَولَتِ دَرویشان است

خُسرُوان قِبلهٔ حاجاتِ جَهانند ولی
سَبَبَش بَندِگیِ حَضرَتِ دَرویشان است

روی مقصود که شاهان به دُعا می‌طَلبند
مَظهَرَش آینهٔ طَلعَتِ دَرویشان است

از کَران تا به کَران لَشکرِ ظُلم است وَلی
از اَزَل تا به اَبَد فُرصَتِ دَرویشان است

ای تَوانگَر مَفُروش این همه نَخوَت که تو را
سَر و زَر در کَنَفِ هِمَّتِ دَرویشان است

گَنجِ قارون که فرو می‌شَوَد از قَهر هَنوز
خوانده باشی که هم از غیرَتِ دَرویشان است

FIFTEEN

The garden of highest paradise is the dervishes' retreat.
The source of magnificence lies in serving dervishes.

The treasure of seclusion, with its magical wonders,
is won only under the merciful gaze of dervishes.

The palace of paradise, where angels seek to serve,
is but a glimpse from their pleasure-field.

The philosopher's stone that turns a black heart to gold
is the intimate company of dervishes.

The sun dips his crown of grandeur before the greatness
that is found in their retinue.

That wealth which we know can never decay—
listen, simply put, it is the wealth of dervishes.

Kings are the focal point of the world's needs
because they are slaves in the presence of dervishes.

The face that kings desire and seek with prayer
is found mirrored in the face of dervishes.

From one border to the other rides the army of cruelty, but
from before creation to beyond time is the domain of dervishes.

O rich one, don't peddle your pride, for your head and your gold
are sheltered by their spiritual power.

Because of God's wrath Qárún's treasure still stinks through the earth.
You may read that this, too, was the zealous work of dervishes.

حـافظ اَر آب حیـاتِ اَزَلـی مـی‌خواهـی
مَنبَعَش خاكِ درِ خَلوَتِ دَرویشان است

بنـدهٔ آصِـفِ عَـهدَم کـه درین سَـلطَنَتَش
صـورتِ خواجِـگی و سـیرتِ دَرویشان است

Háfiz, if you want the water of eternal life,
its source is the dust at the doorway of the dervishes' retreat.

I am the slave of the Ásaf of our time, for in this, his reign,
he has the face of a lord and the heart of a dervish.

شانزده

روزگاری‌ست که سودای بُتان دینِ من است
غمِ این کار نِشاطِ دلِ غمگینِ من است

دیدنِ روی تو را دیدهٔ جان‌بین باید
وین کجا مَرتَبهٔ چَشمِ جَهان بینِ من است

یارِ من باش که زیبِ فَلَک و زینَتِ دَهر
از مَهِ روی تو و اَشکِ چو پروینِ من است

تا مَرا عشقِ تو تَعلیمِ سُخَن گفتن کرد
خلق را وِردِ زبان مَدحَت و تَحسینِ من است

دَولَتِ فَقر خُدایا به من ارزانی دار
کاین کرامَت سَبَبِ حِشمَت و تَمکینِ من است

واعِظِ شَحنه شناس این عَظمَت گو مَفُروش
زان که مَنزلگهِ سُلطان دلِ مِسکینِ من است

یا رَب این کَعبهٔ مَقصود تَماشاگه کیست
که مُغیلانِ طریقَش گُل و نَسرینِ من است

حافظ از حِشمَتِ پرویز دِگر قصّه مَخوان
که لَبَش جُرعه‌کَشِ خُسرُوِ شیرینِ من است

SIXTEEN

For some time passionate idolatry has been my faith.
The pain of this practice is the joy of my sad heart.

One must have a soul-seeing eye to see your face.
How could my world-seeing eye be of this rank?

Be my love, for time's ornaments and heaven's beauty
come from the moon of your face and my tears like the Pleiades.

Ever since my love for you taught me to speak
people always shower me with praise and admiration.

O God, grant me the riches of poverty,
for this grace is the source of my dignity and magnificence.

Tell the preacher, friend to the watchman, to not peddle this grandeur,
for the house of the King is my poor heart.

O lord, whose vista is this Ka'ba I seek?
The briars of its way are my rose and jonquil.

Háfiz, don't tell another story about the pomp of Parviz,
for his lip is but the wine-taster of my sweet king.

هفده

خوشتر ز عیش و صحبت و باغ و بهار چیست
ساقی کجاست گو سبب انتظار چیست

هر وقت خوش که دست دهد مغتنم شمار
کس را وقوف نیست که انجام کار چیست

پیوند عمر بسته به مویی‌ست هوش دار
غمخوار خویش باش غم روزگار چیست

معنیّ آب زندگی و روضهٔ ارم
جز طرف جویبار و می خوشگوار چیست

مستور و مست هر دو چو از یک قبیله‌اند
ما دل به عشوهٔ که دهیم اختیار چیست

راز درون پرده چه داند فلک خموش
ای مدّعی نزاع تو با پرده‌دار چیست

سهو و خطای بنده گرش اعتبار نیست
معنیّ عفو و رحمت آمرزگار چیست

زاهد شراب کوثر و حافظ پیاله خواست
تا در میانه خواستهٔ کردگار چیست

SEVENTEEN

What is more joyous than pleasure, intimacy, the garden, and spring?
Where is the saqí? Ask, "Why are we waiting?"

Hoard each joyous moment that comes to you.
No one knows how it all will end.

Our graft to life is tied with a strand of hair. Be aware.
Take care of yourself. What does fate matter?

What is the meaning of the water of life and the garden of Iram
but delicious wine and the edge of this stream?

Since the upright man is kin to the stumbling drunk,
to whose sultry glance should we give our heart? Is there a choice?

What does heaven know of the veiled secret? O impostor,
be quiet. What is your quarrel with the veil-keeper?

My oversights and mistakes are not counted as a sin. And if they were
isn't God named The All-Forgiving?

The ascetic thirsts for the wine of heaven's fountain
and Háfiz wants his cup refilled. Who knows which God prefers?

هجده

زاهدِ ظاهر پَرَست از حالِ ما آگاه نیست
در حقِ ما هرچه گوید جایِ هیچ اِکراه نیست

در طَریقت هرچه پیشِ سالک آید خیر اوست
در صِراطِ مُستَقیم ای دل کسی گُمراه نیست

تا چه بازی رُخ نَماید بیدَقی خواهیم راند
عَرصهٔ شَطرَنجِ رِندان را مَجالِ شاه نیست

چیست این سَقفِ بُلَندِ سادهٔ بسیار نَقش
زین مُعَمّا هیچ دانا در جَهان آگاه نیست

این چه اِستغناست یا رَب وین چه قادِر حاکم است
کاین همه زخمِ نَهان هست و مَجالِ آه نیست

صاحبِ دیوانِ ما گویی نمی‌داند حساب
کاندَرین طُغرا نِشانِ حِسبَةًلله نیست

هرکه خواهد گو بیا و هر چه خواهد گو بگو
کِبر و ناز و حاجِب و دَربان بدین دَرگاه نیست

هر چه هست از قامتِ ناسازِ بی‌اندام ماست
ور نه تَشریفِ تو بر بالایِ کَس کوتاه نیست

بر درِ میخانه رفتن کارِ یک رَنگان بُوَد
خود فُروشان را به کویِ می فُروشان راه نیست

بندهٔ پیرِ خَراباتم که لُطفَش دایم است
ور نه لطفِ شیخ و زاهد گاه هست و گاه نیست

حافظ ار بَر صَدر نَنشیند ز عالی مَشرَبیست
عاشقِ دُردی‌کِش اَندَر بَندِ مال و جاه نیست

EIGHTEEN

The ascetic who worships appearances knows nothing of my state.
I don't resent anything he says about me.

On the path of truth, whatever happens to the seeker is for his own good.
O heart, on the straight road no one gets lost.

To see what move the rook will make, I will advance a pawn.
On the chessboard of the rends there is no chance at the king.

What is this high vault, plain by day and filled with constellations by night?
In all the world no wise one understands this enigma.

What is this needlessness, O lord, and who is this powerful ruler?
There are so many hidden wounds and no way to sigh.

You could say our bookkeeper doesn't know the rules
because his decree lacks the seal that says "If it is God's will."

Whoever wants to come, let him come. Whatever he wants to say, let him say.
There is no conceit or showing off, no guard or door-keeper in this court.

Whatever has fallen short is due to my inadequate stature
because your robe of honor fits everyone.

Only the sincere ones know the way to the tavern door.
Those who sell themselves cannot find the wine-seller's alleyway.

I am the slave of the tavern elder, whose generosity is everlasting—
unlike the shaikh and preacher, who are sometimes generous, sometimes not.

If Háfiz doesn't sit in the high seat, it's because of his noble nature.
The dreg-drinking lover cares nothing for riches or rank.

نوزده

بَحریست بَحرِ عِشق که هیچَش کَناره نیست
آنجا جُز آن که جان بِسپارند چاره نیست

هَرگَه که دِل به عِشق دَهی خوش دَمی بُوَد
در کارِ خِیر حاجَتِ هیچ اِستِخاره نیست

فُرصَت شِمُر طَریقهٔ رِندی که این نشان
چون راهِ گَنج بَر هَمه کَس آشکاره نیست

ما را ز مَنعِ عَقل مَتَرسان و می بیار
کان شَحنه در وِلایَتِ ما هیچ کاره نیست

او را به چَشمِ پاك تَوان دید چون هِلال
هَر دیده جایِ جِلوهٔ آن ماه پاره نیست

از چَشمِ خود بِپُرس که ما را که میکُشد
جانا گُناهِ طالِع و جُرمِ سِتاره نیست

نَگرفت در تو گِریهٔ حافِظ به هیچ رو
حیرانِ آن دِلَم که کَم از سَنگِ خاره نیست

NINETEEN

The sea of love is a sea that has no shore.
There, you can only give up your soul.

Whenever you give your heart to love it is a joyous moment.
For auspicious deeds there is no need for divination.

Avail yourself of the rend's way, for this mark,
like the road to hidden treasure, is not plain to everyone.

Don't frighten us with reason's prohibitions, and bring wine,
for that watchman has no authority in our province.

One can see him with a pure eye, like the new moon.
Not every eye can hold that crescent's beauty.

Ask your own eyes who is killing us. O soul,
it is not the sin of ascendants and the crime of stars.

You are unaffected by the cry of Háfiz.
I am perplexed at that heart, hard as granite.

بیست

حاصلِ کارگهِ کون و مکان این همه نیست
باده پیش آر که اسبابِ جهان این همه نیست

از دل و جان شرفِ صحبتِ جانان غرض است
همه آن است وگرنه دل و جان این همه نیست

منّتِ سِدره و طوبی ز پیِ سایه مکش
که چو خوش بنگری ای سروِ روان این همه نیست

دولت آن است که بی خونِ دل آید به کنار
ور نه با سعی و عمل باغِ جنان این همه نیست

پنج روزی که در این مرحله مهلت داری
خوش بیاسای زمانی که زمان این همه نیست

بر لبِ بحرِ فنا منتظریم ای ساقی
فرصتی دان که ز لب تا به دهان این همه نیست

زاهد ایمن مشو از بازی غیرت زنهار
که رَه از صومعه تا دیرِ مغان این همه نیست

نامِ حافظ رقمِ نیک پذیرفت ولی
پیشِ رندان رقمِ سود و زیان این همه نیست

TWENTY

What is made in the workshop of the universe, all this is nothing.
Bring out the wine, for the goods of the world are nothing.

Heart and soul seek the honor of intimacy with the beloved.
That is everything. Otherwise, the heart and soul are nothing.

Don't grow indebted to the trees of heaven for the sake of shade,
for when you look closely, O flowing cypress, they are nothing.

Good fortune comes without spilling blood from the heart;
otherwise, with effort and practice, heaven's garden is nothing.

You have five days of respite in this waystation.
Rest easily for a time, because time is nothing.

We wait at the edge of the sea of annihilation. O saqi,
grasp the chance, for the distance between the lip and the mouth is nothing.

Ascetic, beware, don't grow complacent in your zeal,
for the distance between your cloister and the Magi's monastery, this is nothing.

The name of Háfiz has become highly distinguished, but
among rends, the distinction between profit and loss is nothing.

بیست و یک

عِیبِ رِندان مَکُن ای زاهِدِ پاکیزه سِرشت
که گُناهِ دِگران بَر تو نَخواهَند نوشت

مَن اگر نیکَم و گَر بَد تو بُرو خود را باش
هَر کَسی آن دِرَوَد عاقِبَتِ کار که کِشت

هَمه کَس طالبِ یارَند چه هُشیار و چه مَست
هَمه جا خانهٔ عِشق است چه مَسجد چه کِنِشت

سَرِ تَسلیمِ مَن و خِشتِ دَرِ میکده‌ها
مُدَّعی گر نَکُنَد فَهمِ سُخَن گو سَر و خِشت

نا اُمیدَم مَکُن از سابقهٔ لُطفِ اَزَل
تو چه دانی که پَسِ پَردِه که خوب است و که زِشت

نه مَن از پَردهٔ تَقوا به در اُفتادَم و بَس
پِدَرَم نیز بهشتِ اَبَد از دَستِ بِهِشت

گَر نَهادَت هَمه این است زَهی نیک نَهاد
وَر سِرشتَت هَمه این است زَهی خوب سِرِشت

حافظا روزِ اَجَل گَر به کَفِ آری جامی
یِکسَر از کویِ خَرابات بَرَندَت به بهشت

TWENTY-ONE

O holier-than-thou ascetic, don't criticize the rends
for the sins of others won't be charged to your account.

Whether I am good or evil, just mind your own business.
In the end each will reap what he has sown.

Everyone, sober or drunk, is a seeker of the friend.
Every place, whether mosque or temple, is the house of love.

I surrender and lay my head on the tavern's threshold.
If the impostor doesn't understand this, tell him to lay his head in the grave.

Don't make me lose hope of the grace God promised us.
How can you know who is good and who is evil behind the curtain?

I'm not the only one who has been exiled from the sanctuary of virtue.
My father also let eternal paradise slip from his hands.

If you are righteous by nature, congratulations!
And if you are as you claim, good for you!

O Háfiz, if, on the day of your death, you can grasp a winecup
from this tavern's alleyway you'll go straight to heaven.

بیست و دو

دیدی که یار جُز سَرِ جَور و ستَم نداشت
بِشکَست عَهد واز غَمِ ما هیچ غَم نداشت

یا رَب مَگیرَش اَر چه دلِ چون کبوتَرَم
اَفکَند و کُشت و عِزَّتِ صَیدِ حَرَم نداشت

بَر مَن جَفا زِ بَختِ مَن آمَد وَگَرنَه یار
حاشا که رَسمِ لُطف و طَریقِ کَرَم نداشت

با این هَمه هَر آن که نه خواری کشید از او
هَر جا که رفت هیچ کَسَش مُحتَرَم نَداشت

ساقی بیار باده وُ با مُحتَسِب بگو
اِنکارِ ما مَکُن که چُنین جامِ جَم نداشت

هُر راهرو که رَه به حَریمِ دَرَش نَبُرد
مِسکین بُرید وادی و رَه در حَرَم نداشت

حافظ بِبَر تو گویِ فَصاحَت که مُدَّعی
هیچَش هُنَر نَبود و خَبَر نیز هَم نداشت

TWENTY-TWO

You saw that my love meant nothing but injustice and abuse?
She broke her promise, and my pain caused her no pain.

She threw down and killed my heart, as it if were a pigeon.
O Lord, spare her, although Your law forbids hunting in the sanctuary.

These misfortunes came to me from my bad luck, otherwise,
God forbid, she might be thought ungentle or unkind.

Nevertheless, he who never drew her scorn
was not respected, no matter where he went.

Saqi, bring wine, and tell the pious magistrate,
"Don't deny us. Not even Jamshid had a cup like this."

Each traveler who didn't find the road to the sacred enclosure
wandered wretched in the desert and never found its door.

Háfiz, take the prize for eloquence, for the impostor
had no skill and knew nothing.

بیست و سه

شَرْبَتی از لَبِ لَعْلَش نَچشیدیم و بِرَفت
رویِ مَه پِیکرِ او سیر نَدیدیم و بِرَفت

گویی از صُحبتِ ما نیک به تَنگ آمده بود
بار بَربَست و به گَردَش نَرسیدیم و بِرَفت

بَس که ما فاتِحه وُ حِرزِ یَمانی خواندیم
وَز پِی‌اش سورهٔ اِخلاص دَمیدیم و بِرَفت

عِشوه می‌داد که از کویِ اِرادَت نَرَویم
دیدی آخِرکه چُنین عِشوه خریدیم و بِرَفت

شُد چَمان در چَمَنِ حُسن و لطافتِ لیکَن
در گُلِستانِ وِصالَش نَچَمیدیم و بِرَفت

همچو حافظ هَمه شب ناله و زاری کردیم
کای دَریغا به وِداعَش نَرسیدیم و بِرَفت

TWENTY-THREE

We didn't taste a drop from her ruby lip and she left.
We didn't gaze long enough at her beauty and she left.

Perhaps she had tired of our company.
She packed her things, we couldn't overtake her, and she left.

We recited holy suras and blew prayers after her
and she left.

Her sultry glance rooted us in the alley of devotion.
In the end, you saw how deeply we bought that glance, and she left.

She strolled in the field of grace and beauty but
we didn't go to meet her in the garden of union and she left.

We wailed and wept all night, just like Háfiz,
for alas, we were too late to say goodbye and she left.

بیست و چهار

ساقی بیا که یار ز رُخ پَرده بَرگِرِفت
کارِ چِراغِ خَلوَتیان باز دَرگِرِفت

آن شمعِ سَر گِرِفته دِگَر چِهره بَرفُروخت
وین پیرِ سالخورده جَوانی ز سَر گِرِفت

آن عِشوه داد عِشق که مُفتی ز رَه بِرَفت
وان لُطف کرد دوست که دُشمَن حَذَر گِرِفت

زِنهار از آن عِبارتِ شیرینِ دِلفَریب
گویی که پِسته‌ای تو سُخَن دَر شِکَر گِرِفت

بارِ غَمی که خاطرِ ما خَسته کرده بود
عیسی دَمی خُدا بِفِرستاد و برگِرِفت

هر سَروقَد که بَر مَه و خور حُسن می‌فروخت
چون تو درآمدی پیِ کاری دِگَر گِرِفت

زین قِصّهٔ هَفت گُنبَدِ اَفلاک پُرصداست
کوته نَظَر ببین که سُخَن مُختَصَر گِرِفت

حافظ تو این سُخَن ز که آموختی که بَخت
تَعویذ کرد شِعرِ تَو را و به زَر گِرِفت

TWENTY-FOUR

Saqi, come. The friend has taken the veil from her face.
The light of the solitary ones has been rekindled.

That candle, once beheaded, lit is face again
and burned the grey years from this old man.

Love's sultry glance drove virtue from the road.
She was so kind that the enemy stepped aside.

Pay attention to that sweet, charming message.
It's as if your mouth wrapped speech in sugar.

For the burden of grief which struck my heart
God sent a messiah who took it away.

Each cypress peddling its beauty to the sun and moon
sat down quietly when you came in.

The seven domes of heaven echo with this story.
Look at the near-sighted ones who didn't think it worth repeating!

Háfiz, from whom did you learn these words, that the friend
has wrapped your verse in gold to wear around her neck?

بیست و پنج

صُبحدَم مُرغِ چَمَن با گُل نوخاسته گُفت
نَاز کم کُن که دَر این باغ بَسی چون تو شِکُفت

گُل بِخَندید که از راست نَرَنجیم وَلی
هیچ عاشِق سُخَنِ سَخت به مَعشوق نَگُفت

گَر طَمَع داری از آن جامِ مُرَصَّع می لَعل
ای بَسا دُر که به نوکِ مُژهات باید سُفت

تا اَبَد بوی مُحَبَّت به مَشامَش نَرِسَد
هَر که خاکِ دَرِ میخانه به رُخساره نَرُفت

در گُلِستانِ اِرَم دوش چو از لُطفِ هَوا
زُلفِ سُنبُل به نَسیمِ سَحَری می‌آشُفت

گفتم ای مَسنَدِ جَم جامِ جَهان بینَت کو
گفت اَفسوس که آن دَولَتِ بیدار بِخُفت

سُخَنِ عِشق نَه آنَست که آید به زَبان
ساقیا می دِه و کوتاه کُن این گُفت و شِنُفت

اَشکِ حافظ خِرَد و صَبر به دَریا اَنداخت
چه کُند سوزِ غَمِ عِشق نَیارَست نَهُفت

TWENTY-FIVE

At dawn the nightingale spoke to the newly-risen rose:
"Don't put on airs, for many like you have blossomed in this garden."

The rose laughed, "The truth does not offend, but never
has a lover spoken harshly to his love."

If you desire red wine from the jeweled cup
your eyelash must pierce pearl and ruby.

For all eternity the scent of love will elude the one
whose cheek has not swept the dust of the tavern threshold.

Last night in the rose garden of Iram
when a gentle breeze tousled the hyacinth's curls,

I said, "O throne of Jamshid, where is your world-seeing cup?"
It said, "Alas, that glorious realm is gone."

Talk of love is beyond words.
O sáqí, give me wine, and cut short this bickering.

The tears of Háfiz threw wisdom and patience to the sea.
What to do? Love's burning pain cannot be hidden.

بیست و شش

ای هُدهُدِ صَبا به سَبا می‌فرِستَمَت
بِنگَر که از کُجا به کُجا می‌فِرِستَمَت

حیف است طایری چو تو در خاکدانِ غَم
زیـن جـا بـه آشیانِ وَفا می‌فِرِستَمَت

در راهِ عشق مَرحَلهٔ قُرب و بُعد نیست
می‌بینَمَت عَیـان و دُعـا می‌فِرِستَمَت

هـر صُبـح و شـام قـافله‌ای از دُعای خیر
در صُحبَتِ شُمال و صَبا می‌فِرِستَمَت

تا لَشکَرِ غَمَت نَکُنَد مُلکِ دل خَراب
جـانِ عَزیزِ خـود به نَـوا می‌فِرِستَمَت

ای غایب از نَظَر که شُدی هَمنشینِ دل
می‌گویَمَت دُعـا و ثَنا می‌فِرِستَمَت

در رویِ خود تَفَرُّجِ صُنعِ خُدای کن
کآیینهٔ خدای نَـما می‌فِرِستَمَت

تا مُطرِبان زِ شَوقِ مَنَت آگَهی دِهَند
قَولَ و غَزَل به ساز و نَوا می‌فِرِستَمَت

ساقی بیا که هاتِفِ غِیبَم به مُژده گُفت
بـا دَردِ صَبر کُن که دَوا می‌فِرِستَمَت

حافظ سُرودِ مَجلسِ ما ذکرِ خیرِ توست
بِشتاب هـان که اَسب و قَبا می‌فِرِستَمَت

TWENTY-SIX

O hoopoe of the dawn wind, I send you to Sheba.
See how far away I am sending you!

It's a shame, a bird like you in this crumbling ruin of sorrow.
From here I send you to the nest of loyalty.

On the path of love there is no station of near-and-far.
I can see you clearly, and send you greetings.

Morning and evening I send you a caravan of prayers
with the east wind and the north wind.

To prevent the army of sorrow from laying waste to the kingdom of my heart
I send my dear life to you as a hostage.

O hidden one who is now my heart's companion,
I send you greetings.

In your own face view God's creative power
for I send you the God-revealing mirror.

So that the minstrels may tell you of my desire
I send you lyric and ghazal, with music and melody.

Saqi, bring wine, for an invisible voice brought me good news:
"Be patient with pain, for I send you a remedy."

Háfiz, our assembly sings of your goodness.
Hurry up. I send you a horse and tunic.

بیست و هفت

ای غایب از نَظَر به خُدا می‌سپارَمَت
جانَم بِسوختی و به دِل دوست دارَمَت

تا دامَنِ کَفَن نَکِشَم زیرِ پای خاك
باوَر مَكُن كه دست زِ دامَن بدارَمَت

مِحرابِ ابرویَت بِنما تا سَحَرگَهی
دستِ دُعا بَرآرَم و در گَردَن آرَمَت

گَر بایدَم شُدن سویِ هاروتِ بابِلی
صَد گونه جادویی بِكُنَم تا بیارَمَت

خواهم که پیش میرَمَت ای بی وَفا طَبیب
بیمار بازپُرس كه در انتِظارَمَت

صَد جویِ آب بَسته‌ام از دیده بَر کِنار
بَر بویِ تُخمِ مِهر كه در دِل بِكارَمَت

خونَم بِریخت وَز غَمِ عِشقَم خَلاص داد
مِنَّت پَذیرِ غَمزهٔ خَنجَر گُذارَمَت

بارَم دِه از كَرَم بَرِ خود تا به سوزِ دِل
در پایِ دَم به دَم گُهَر از دیده بارَمَت

حافظ شراب و شاهد و رِندی نه وضعِ توست
فِی‌الجُمله می‌کنی و فُرو می‌گذارَمَت

TWENTY-SEVEN

O you who have left me, I entrust you to God.
You burned my soul and with all my heart I love you.

Until I drag the hem of my shroud under the earth
don't believe I will ever let go of the hem of your skirt.

Show me the arched niche of your eyebrows so that at dawn
I may raise my arms in prayer and clasp your neck.

Even if I must seek out Harut of Babylon,
I will cast a hundred spells to conjure you.

I want to die near you. O disloyal healer,
visit the sick one again, I am waiting.

I have cried a hundred streams across my breast
hoping to water the seed of kindness in your heart.

My spilled blood freed me from the pain of love.
I am grateful to the dagger of your glance.

Be kind, grant me an audience, so that with burning heart
my eyes can constantly rain pearls at your feet.

Háfiz, wine and the beloved and the rend's way are not for you,
but you pursue them all and I overlook it.

بیست و هشت

حُسنَت به اِتِّفاقِ مَلاحَت جَهان گِرِفت
آری به اِتِّفاق جَهان می‌توان گِرِفت

اِفشای رازِ خَلوَتِ ما خواست کَرد شَمع
شُکرِ خُدا که سِرِّ دِلَش در زَبان گِرِفت

زین آتَشِ نَهُفته که در سینهٔ مَن است
خورشید شُعله ایست که در آسمان گِرِفت

می‌خواست گُل که دَم زَنَد از رَنگ و بویِ دوست
از غِیرَتِ صَبا نَفَسَش در دَهان گِرِفت

آسوده بَر کِنار چو پَرگار می‌شُدَم
دوران چو نُقطه عاقِبَتَم در میان گِرِفت

آن روز شَوقِ ساغَرِ می خَرمَنَم بَسوخت
کاتش زِ عَکسِ عارِضِ ساقی در آن گِرِفت

خواهَم شُدَن به کویِ مُغان آستین فشان
زین فِتنه‌ها که دامَنِ آخِرِ زَمان گِرِفت

می خور که هَر که آخِرِ کارِ جَهان بِدید
از غَم سَبُک بَرآمد و رَطلِ گِران گِرِفت

بَر بَرگِ گُل به خونِ شَقایق نوشته‌اند
کان کَس که پُخته شُد می چون اَرغَوان گِرِفت

فُرصَت نِگَر که فِتنه چو دَر عالَم اوفتاد
صوفی به جام می زَد و از غَم کَران گِرِفت

حافظ چو آبِ لُطف ز نَظمِ تو می‌چِکَد
حاسِد چگونه نُکته تَوانَد بَران گِرِفت

TWENTY-EIGHT

Your beauty and grace, together, conquered the world.
Yes, unity can conquer the world.

The candle wanted to reveal the secret of my seclusion.
Thank God that the secret in its heart burned its tongue.

Compared to this fire hidden in my heart
the sun is but a tiny flame in the sky.

The rose wanted to boast that its color and scent were like the friend's
but the jealous dawn wind took its breath away.

Like one leg of a compass I walked calmly along the edge.
Now I am encircled by time and fate.

My love for the cup of wine destroyed my life the day
that the reflection of the saqi's face set it ablaze.

Given the chaos of this end of days
I want to go to the Magi's alleyway, dancing.

Drink wine, for whoever foresaw how the world ends
put down his burden of sorrow and picked up a weighty cup.

On the petal of the rose it is written in poppy-blood
that he who has ripened drinks the darkest wine.

Seize the moment, for when there is trouble in the world
the Sufi picks up the cup of wine and leaves sorrow behind.

Háfiz, because the nectar of grace drips from your verse
how can the envious find fault in it?

بیست و نه

شنیده‌ام سُخَنی خوش که پیرِ کَنعان گُفت
فِراقِ یار نه آن می‌کُنَد که بِتوان گُفت

حَدیثِ هَولِ قیامَت که گُفت واعظِ شَهر
کِنایَتی‌ست که از روزگارِ هِجران گُفت

نِشانِ یارِ سَفَر کرده از که پُرسَم باز
که هَر چِه گُفت بَریدِ صَبا پَریشان گُفت

فَغان که آن مَهِ نامِهرَبانِ مِهر گُسَل
به تَرکِ صُحبَتِ یارانِ خود چه آسان گُفت

مَن و مَقامِ رِضا بعد ازین و شُکرِ رَقیب
که دِل به دَردِ تو خو کرد و تَرکِ دَرمان گُفت

گِرِه به باد مَزَن گر چه بَر مُراد رَوَد
که این سُخَن به مَثَل باد با سُلیمان گُفت

به مُهلَتی که سِپِهرَت دِهَد زِ راه مَرو
تو را که گُفت که این زالِ تَرکِ دَستان گُفت

غَمِ کُهَن به مِی سالخورده دَفعِ کنید
که تُخمِ خوشدِلی این است پیرِ دِهقان گُفت

مَزَن زِ چون و چِرا دَم که بَندهٔ مُقبِل
قَبول کرد به جان هَر سُخَن که جانان گُفت

که گُفتِ حافظ از اندیشهٔ تو آمد باز
مَن این نَگُفته‌اَم آن کَس که گُفت بُهتان گُفت

TWENTY-NINE

I heard this tale from the Elder of Canaan:
"There are no words for feeling far away from the friend."

The town preacher's homily about the terror of Resurrection Day
gave just a hint about such days of separation.

Who can tell me news of my love who left?
Because everything the dawn wind said was nonsense.

Alas! Look at how easily my unkind, enemy-loving beloved
abandoned the companionship of her own friends!

I surrender. From now on I accept her guardian.
My heart grew accustomed to the pain of loving you and gave up on a cure.

Don't rely on the wind, even if it blows in your favor.
This was the advice the ant gave Solomon.

If life gives you a moment's respite, don't stray from the path.
Who said that this crone has given up lying?

Drown your old sorrow with ancient wine,
for this is the seed of happiness. The village elder said so.

Don't ask why or how, for the one who has been accepted by God
accepts with his soul every word the beloved said.

Who said that Háfiz gave up thinking about you?
I never said this, and whoever said this slanders me.

سی

زان یارِ دِلنَوازَم شُکریست با شِکایَت
گر نُکتِه‌دانِ عِشقی بِشنو تو این حِکایَت

بی مُزد بود و مِنَّت هر خِدَمتی که کَردَم
یا رَب مَباد کَس را مَخدومِ بی‌عِنایَت

رِندانِ تِشنِه لَب را آبی نمی‌دهد کَس
گویی وَلی شِناسان رفتند ازین وِلایَت

هر چَند بُردی آبَم روی از دَرَت نَتابَم
جَور از حَبیب خوشتَر کز مُدَّعی رِعایَت

در زُلفِ چون کَمَندَش ای دِل مَپیچ کان جا
سَرها بُریده بینی بی‌جُرم و بی‌جِنایَت

چَشمَت به غَمزه ما را خون خورد و می‌پَسندی
جانا رَوا نَباشد خون ریز را حِمایَت

در این شَبِ سیاهَم گُم گَشت راهِ مَقصود
از گوشه‌ای بُرون آی ای کوکبِ هِدایَت

از هَر طَرَف که رَفتَم جُز وَحشَتَم نَیَفزود
زِنهار ازین بیابان وین راهِ بی‌نِهایَت

این راه را نِهایَت صورَت کُجا تَوان بَست
کش صَد هِزار مَنزِل بیش است در بِدایَت

عِشقَت رِسَد به فَریاد اَر خود به سانِ حافِظ
قُرآن زِ بَر بِخوانی در چارده روایَت

THIRTY

Toward my gracious friend I feel gratitude—with complaint.
If you understand love's subtleties, pay attention to this story.

I offered my service without pay or expectation.
O lord, may no one have an ungrateful master.

No one offers a cup to the thirsty rends,
as if those who could recognize a friend of God have all left town.

Although you have disgraced me I won't turn my face from your door.
The friend's blow is lovelier than the hypocrite's respect.

O heart, don't ask questions about the lasso of her hair, for there
you'll see the severed heads of hundreds who are innocent of crime or offense.

Your flirtatious eyes drank my heart's blood—and you like it!
O soul, it is unjust to protect the blood-thirsty.

In this dark night I lost my way to my destination.
O guiding star, come out from your hiding place!

Wherever I turned I found nothing but more terror.
Beware of this wilderness and this road without end.

How can you imagine an end to this road
that has more than 100,000 stages before it begins?

Only love will save you—even if, like Háfiz,
you can recite by heart all fourteen versions of the Qur'an.

سی و یک

روزِ وَصلِ دوستـداران یاد باد
یـاد بـاد آن روزگاران یاد باد

کامَم از تَلخیِ غَم چـون زَهر گشت
بانگِ نوشِ شادخواران یاد باد

گر چه یاران فارِغَند از یادِ من
از مـن ایشـان را هِـزاران یـاد بـاد

مُبتَلا گَشتَم دَرین بَند و بَلا
کـوشِـشِ آن حَـق گُزاران یاد بـاد

گر چِه صَد رود است در چَشمَم مُدام
زِنـدِه رود و بــاغ کـاران یاد بـاد

رازِ حافظ بَعد اَزین ناگُفته مـاند
اَی دَریــغــا راز داران یــاد بـاد

THIRTY-ONE

Remember the day of union with the friends.
Remember those times, remember.

From bitter sorrow my mouth became like poison.
Remember the revelers' cry of "Drink!"

The friends are free of the memory of me
although I remember them a thousand times.

I was overtaken in these bonds of calamity.
Remember the efforts of those loyal friends.

Although there are always a hundred rivers in my eye
remember the Zindehrúd, and those who plant gardens.

After this Háfiz's secret will remain unspoken.
Alas, remember those who keep the secrets.

سی و دو

هر آن کاو خاطِری مَجموع و یاری نازَنین دارد
سَعادت هَمدَم او گشت و دَولت هَمنِشین دارد

حَریمِ عشق را دَرگَه بَسی بالاتر از عَقل است
کسی آن آستان بوسَد که جان دَر آستین دارد

دهانِ تَنگِ شیرینَت مَگر مُهرِ سُلیمان است
که نَقشِ خاتَمِ لَعلَش جَهان زیرِ نِگین دارد

لَبِ لَعل و خَطِ مشکین چو اینَش هست آتَش نیست
بِنازَم دِلبَرِ خود را که حُسنَش آن و این دارد

چو بَر روی زَمین باشی تَوانایی غَنیمَت دان
که دوران ناتَوانی‌ها بَسی زیرِ زَمین دارد

به خواری مَنگَر ای مُنعِم ضَعیفان و نَحیفان را
که صَدرِ مَجلِسِ عِزَّت فَقیرِ رَه نِشین دارد

بَلاگردانِ جان و دل دُعای مُستَمندان است
که بینَد خیر از آن خَرمن که نَنگ از خوشِه چین دارد

صَبا از عشقِ من رَمزی بگو با آن شَهِ خوبان
که صَد جَمشید و کِیخُسرو غُلامِ کَمترین دارد

اگر گویَد نمی‌خواهم چو حافظ عاشقی مُفلِس
بگوییدش که سُلطانی گِدایی هَمنِشین دارد

THIRTY-TWO

Everyone who has a clear mind and a lovely friend
is an intimate of bliss and a companion to good fortune.

The threshold of love's sanctuary lies far above that of reason.
To kiss that threshold you must be ready to scatter your life like coins.

Is your small, sweet mouth the seal of Solomon?
The image on its ruby bezel rules all the world.

The boy with ruby lips lacks a darkening beard.
I boast of my beloved: he has both.

Do as much as you can while you walk the earth,
for under the earth time holds many who can do nothing.

O rich one, do not look with contempt on the weak and feeble,
for in the assembly's seat of honor sits the roadside pauper.

The prayers of the needy keep disaster from soul and body,
how will you see a full harvest if you scorn the gleaners?

Wind, tell a secret of my love to that king of beauties,
who among his slaves has a hundred Khusraus and Jamshids,

and if he says, "I do not want a poor lover like Háfiz,"
tell him true kings sit with wandering beggars.

سی و سه

سالها دِل طَلَبِ جامِ جَم از ما می‌کرد
آن چه خود داشت ز بیگانه تَمَنّا می‌کرد

گوهَری کَز صَدَفِ کَون و مَکان بیرون است
طلَب از گم شُدگانِ رَهِ دَریا می‌کرد

مُشکِلِ خویش بَرِ پیرِ مُغان بُردَم دوش
کو به تأییدِ نَظَر حَلِّ مُعَمّا می‌کرد

دیدَمَش خُرَّم و خَندان قَدَحِ باده به دست
وَندَران آیِنه صَد گونه تَماشا می‌کرد

گفتم این جامِ جَهان بین به تو کی داد حَکیم
گفت آن روز که این گُنبَدِ مینا می‌کرد

گفت آن یار کَزو گَشت سَرِ دار بُلَند
جُرمَش این بود که اَسرار هُویدا می‌کرد

بی دِلی در هَمه اَحوال خُدا با او بود
او نمی‌دیدَش و از دور خدایا می‌کرد

آن هَمه شُعبَدهٔ عَقل که می‌کرد آنجا
سامِری پیشِ عَصا و یَدِ بِیضا می‌کرد

فِیضِ روحُ القُدُس اَر باز مَدَد فَرماید
دیگران هم بِکُنَند آنچه مَسیحا می‌کرد

گُفتَمَش سلسلهٔ زُلفِ بُتان از پی چیست
گفت حافظ گِله‌ای اَز دِلِ شِیدا می‌کرد

THIRTY-THREE

For years my heart asked me for Jamshid's cup.
That which it held it sought from strangers.

It sought the pearl that lies outside the universe's shell
from the lost ones on their way to the sea.

Last night I took my dilemma to the elder of the Magi
that with his vision he could find the answer.

I saw him joyous, smiling, cup of wine in hand,
and in that mirror he saw thousands of images.

I said, "When did the All-Knowing give you this world-seeing cup?"
He said, "The day that He built this dark blue dome."

He said, "That beloved who brought honor to the gallows,
his sin was this: he revealed the secrets.

God always walked with the lost-hearted one
who did not see Him and into the distance called, 'O God!'

All the sleights-of-hand that reason used at the beginning
the sorcerers tried on Moses, to no avail.

If the grace of the Holy Spirit helps again
others may do all that Jesus did."

I asked, "The chains of the idol's hair, what are they for?"
He said, "Háfiz complained of a frenzied heart."

سی و چهار

به سِرِّ جامِ جَم آنگَه نَظَر تَوانی کرد
که خاکِ میکَده کُحلِ بَصَر تَوانی کرد

مَباش بی می و مُطرب که زیرِ طاقِ سپهر
به این تَرانه غَم از دل به دَر تَوانی کرد

گُلِ مُرادِ تو آنگَه نِقاب بُگشاید
که خِدمَتش چو نَسیم سَحَر تَوانی کرد

گدایی در میخانه طُرفه اِکسیریست
گر این عَمَل بِکُنی خاک زَر تَوانی کرد

جَمالِ یار نَدارَد نِقاب و پَرده وَلی
غُبارِ رَه بِنِشان تا نَظَر تَوانی کرد

به عَزمِ مَرحَلهٔ عِشق پیش نِه قَدَمی
که سودها کُنی اَر این سَفَر تَوانی کرد

تو کَز سَرای طَبیعَت نِمی‌رَوی بیرون
کجا به کویِ طَریقَت گُذَر تَوانی کرد

دِلا زِ نورِ هِدایَت گَر آگَهی یابی
چو شَمع خَنده زَنان تَرکِ سَر تَوانی کرد

وَلی تو تا لَبِ مَعشوق و جام می خواهی
طَمَع مَدار که کارِ دِگَر تَوانی کرد

گر این نَصیحَتِ شاهانه بِشنَوی حافظ
به شاهراهِ حَقیقَت گُذَر تَوانی کرد

THIRTY-FOUR

You can understand the secret of Jamshid's cup
when you can turn tavern dust into the kohl of sight.

Don't be without wine and minstrel, for under the sky's arch
with this remedy you can banish pain from your heart.

The rose of your desire will lift its veil
the moment you can serve it like the wind of dawn.

Begging at the tavern door is a wondrous elixir.
If you do this you can turn dust to gold.

My love's beauty has no mask, no veil, but
let the road's dust settle, so you can see.

With your eye on the station of love, step forward.
There is great profit if you can make this journey.

You who never leave the walled house of your nature,
how can you pass through the alley of the way?

O heart, if you become aware of the light that guides,
like the laughing candle you can give up your head,

but as long as you want those lips and the wine cup
don't imagine that you can do anything else.

If you listen to this royal advice, Háfiz,
you can travel the royal road of truth.

سی و پنج

در اَزَل پَرتُوِ حُسنَت زِ تَجَلّی دَم زد
عِشق پیدا شُد و آتَش به هَمه عالَم زد

جلوه‌ای کرد رُخَت دید مَلَک عشق نداشت
عینِ آتَش شُد از این غِیرَت و بر آدَم زد

عَقل می‌خواست کَزان شُعله چراغ اَفروزد
بَرقِ غِیرَت بِدِرَخشید و جَهان بَرهَم زد

مُدَّعی خواست که آیَد به تَماشاگهِ راز
دستِ غِیب آمد و بر سینهٔ نامَحرَم زد

دیگران قُرعهٔ قسمت هَمه بَر عِیش زدند
دلِ غَمدیدهٔ ما بود که هَمّ بر غَم زد

جانِ عِلوی هَوَسِ چاهِ زَنَخدانِ تو داشت
دست در حَلقهٔ آن زُلفِ خَم اَندَر خَم زد

حافظ آن روز طَرَبنامهٔ عشقِ تو نوشت
که قَلَم بر سَرِ اَسبابِ دلِ خُرَّم زد

THIRTY-FIVE

On the eve of creation the ray of your beauty broke forth.
Love appeared and set fire to the universe.

The radiance of your face appeared. Incensed that the angel could not love
it became the essence of fire and struck Adam.

With that flame reason sought to light a lamp.
Your zeal was bolt lightning, and stirred up all the world.

The impostor came to see the secret. He was not kin,
and the hand of the invisible pushed him away.

All the others cast their lots for pleasure.
Our pain-filled heart was the one that cast its lot for sorrow.

The celestial soul sought to drink from the well of your dimple,
and lowered himself on the curved curls of your hair.

Háfiz finished his book on the joy of loving you
the day that he crossed out all that describes a cheerful heart.

سی و شش

اگـر رَوَم زِ پِی‌اَش فِتنه‌ها بَرانگیزد
وَر از طَلَب بِنِشینم به کینـه بَرخیزد

وَ گَر بـه رَهگُذَری یِک دَم از وَفاداری
چـو گَرد در پِی‌اَش اُفتم چو بـاد بُگریزد

وَ گَر کنم طَلَب نیـم بوسه صَد اَفسوسِ
زِحُقّهٔ دَهَنَش چـون شِکَر فُرو ریزَد

مـن آن فَریب که در نَرگسِ تو می‌بینم
بَـس آبروی که بـا خـاكِ رَه بَرآمیزد

فـراز و شیبِ بیابانِ عِشـق دام بلاست
کُجـاست شیردِلی کَز بَلا نَپَرهیزد

تـو عُمر خواه و صَبوری که چَرخِ شُعبَدَه باز
هـزار بـازی ازین طُرفِـه تر بَرانگیزد

بـر آستانـهٔ تَسلیم سَر بنِـه حافظ
کـه گر سِتیـزه کُنی روزگار بِستیزَد

THIRTY-SIX

If I follow her, she stirs up trouble;
and if I sit back, she rises up in anger;

and if on a road, for one moment, in my loyalty,
like dust I follow her, like wind she flees;

and if I seek half a kiss from the jewel-box of her mouth,
hundreds of "So sorry!"s spill down like sugar.

That deceit which I see in your eyes
muddies many a good name with the dust of the road.

The hills and valleys of love's wilderness are the snare of affliction.
Who has a lion's heart, and will not shun affliction?

Seek life and patience, for the great wheel, with its sleight-of-hand,
has a thousand tricks more strange than these.

Háfiz, place your head on the threshold of submission,
for if you pick a fight, fate will fight back.

سی و هفت

هَرکِه شُد مَحرَمِ دِل در حَرَمِ یار بِماند
وَانکِه اَین کار نَدانِست در اِنکار بِماند

اگر از پَرده بُرون شُد دِلِ مَن عیب مَکُن
شُکرِ ایزَد که نَه در پَردهٔ پِندار بِماند

صوفیان واسِتَدَند از گِرُوِ می هَمه رَخت
دَلقِ ما بود که در خانهٔ خَمّار بِماند

خِرقه پوشانِ دِگر مَست گُذَشتَند و گُذَشت
قِصّهٔ ماست که در هَر سَرِ بازار بِماند

هَر مِی لَعل کَزان دَستِ بُلورین سِتَدیم
آب حَسرَت شُد و در چَشمِ گُهَربار بِماند

جُز دِلِ مَن کَز اَزَل تا به اَبَد عاشِق رَفت
جاودان کَس نَشنیدیم که در کار بِماند

از صِدای سُخَنِ عِشق نَدیدَم خوشتر
یادگاری کِه در این گُنبَدِ دَوّار بِماند

گَشت بیمار که چون چَشمِ تو گَردَد نَرگِس
شیوهٔ تو نَشُدَش حاصِل و بیمار بِماند

بِه تَماشاگهِ زُلفَش دِلِ حافِظ روزی
شُد که باز آیَد و جاویدَ گِرِفتار بِماند

THIRTY-SEVEN

Whoever became an intimate of the heart remained in the friend's sanctuary,
and whoever didn't understand remained in denial.

Don't fault my heart if it shed the veil.
Thank God it didn't stay veiled in imagination.

The Sufis redeemed all the clothes they pawned for wine.
Only my coat remained in the tavern.

The other Sufis passed by drunk and unremarked.
Only my story remained the talk of every bazaar.

The ruby wine that we took from that pale hand
turned to pure regret and fell from our eyes like pearls.

Except for my heart, which has been in love from before creation to beyond time,
we have heard of no one else who has been eternal in this work.

I have never seen a more beautiful reminder
than the words of love that linger in this turning dome.

The narcissus grew ill and tried to mimic your sultry eyes.
Your ways were beyond him and he lies sick still.

One day Háfiz's heart went to gaze at his lovely curls.
It meant to return but remained entangled forever.

سی و هشت

دوش دیدَم که مَلایک دَرِ میخانه زَدَند
گِلِ آدَم بِسِرِشتَند و به پیمانه زَدَند

ساکنانِ حَرَمِ سِتر و عِفافِ مَلَکوت
با مَنِ راه نِشین بادهٔ مَستانه زَدَند

آسمان بارِ اَمانَت نَتوانست کِشید
قُرعهٔ کار به نامِ منِ دیوانه زَدَند

جَنگِ هَفتاد و دو مِلَّت هَمه را عُذر بِنه
چون نَدیدَند حَقیقَت رَهِ افسانه زَدَند

شُکرِ ایزَد که میانِ مَن و او صُلح افتاد
صوفیان رَقص کُنان ساغَرِ شُکرانه زَدَند

ما به صَد خَرمَنِ پِندار زِ رَه چون نَرَویم
چون رَهِ آدَمِ بیدار به یک دانه زَدَند

آتش آن نیست که بَر شُعلهٔ او خَندد شَمع
آتش آن است که دَر خَرمَنِ پَروانه زَدَند

کَس چو حافظ نَگُشاد از رُخِ اَندیشه نِقاب
تا سَرِ زُلفِ سُخَن را به قَلَم شانه زَدَند

THIRTY-EIGHT

Last night I saw angels knock on the tavern door.
With wine they kneaded the clay of Adam and molded it into a cup.

Those who live in the veiled and chaste sanctuary of heaven
drank strong wine with me, the wandering beggar.

The sky couldn't bear the burden of His trust
so they cast lots and drew the name of crazy me.

Excuse all the seventy-two nations at war.
They did not see the truth and took the road of fable.

Thank God that peace has fallen between us.
The celestials danced and drank the cup of gratitude.

How can we not be diverted by a thousand thoughts
when they waylaid watchful Adam with a single grain?

Fire is not the candle's laughing flame.
Fire is that which turned the moth to ash.

No one has unveiled the face of thought as well as Háfiz
since men began to comb, with a pen, the curly head of speech.

سی و نه

سَمَن بویان غُبارِ غَم چو بنشینَند بنشانَند
پَری رویانْ قَرار از دل چو بِستیزَند بِستانَند

به فتراکِ جَفا دلها چو بَربَندند بربَندند
زِ زُلفِ عَنبَرین جانها چو بُگشایند بفشانَند

به عُمری یک نَفَس باما چو بنشینَند بَرخیزَند
نَهالِ شَوق در خاطِر چو بَرخیزَند بنشانَند

زِ چَشمَم لَعلِ رُمّانی چو می‌خندند می‌بارند
زِ رویَم رازِ پِنهانی چو می‌بینَند می‌خوانَند

سِرشکِ گوشه گیران را چو دَریابَند دُر یابَند
رُخِ مِهر از سَحَر خیزان نَگردانَند اگر دانَند

دَوای دردِ عاشق را کَسی کو سَهل پِندارد
زِ فِکر آنان که در تَدبیرِ دَرمانَند دَر مانَند

چو منصور از مُرادِ آنان که بَردارند بَر دارند
بِدین دَرگاه حافظ را چو می‌خوانَند می‌رانَند

THIRTY-NINE

When the jasmine-scented ones sit down they settle the dust of sorrow.
When the fairy-faced ones quarrel they steal peace from the heart.

When they ride they strap our hearts to their saddle with capriciousness.
When they let down their perfumed hair they scatter souls.

When they sit with us for one moment in a lifetime they get up.
When they get up they root a sapling of love and longing in the heart.

When they make my eyes rain pomegranate tears they laugh.
When they look they read the hidden secret in my face.

When they discover the tears of the secluded ones they see pearls.
When they understand, they do not turn their face from the love of
    those who rise at dawn.

Who thinks the lover's pain has an easy cure?
Those who seek a remedy will be paralyzed.

Those whose desires bear fruit, like Halláj, stand upon the gallows.
As soon as they call Háfiz to this threshold they send him away.

چهل

واعِظان کاین جِلوه در مِحراب و مِنبَر می‌کُنَند
چون به خَلوَت می‌رَوَند آن کارِ دیگر می‌کُنَند

مُشکِلی دارم زِ دانِشمَندِ مَجلِس بازپُرس
تَوبَه فَرمایان چِرا خود تَوبَه کَمتر می‌کُنَند

گـویـیـا بـاوَر نـمـی‌دارنــد روز داوری
کاین هَمه قَلب و دَغَل در کارِ داور می‌کُنَند

بنده‌ٔ پیرِ خَراباتم که دَرویشانِ او
گنـج را از بـی‌نیـازی خاک بَر سَر می‌کُنَند

یا رَب این نَودولتان را با خَرِ خودشان نشان
کایَن هَمه ناز از غُلامِ تُرک و اَستَر می‌کُنَند

بر دَرِ میخانهٔ عِشـق ای مَلَک تَسبیح گوی
کاندَر آنجا طینتِ آدَم مُخَمَّر می‌کُنَند

حُسنِ بی پایانِ او چَندان که عاشق می‌کُشد
زُمره‌ای دیگر به عِشق از غِیب سَر بَر می‌کُنَند

ای گدای خانِقَه بَرجِه که در دِیرِ مُغان
می‌دهَند آبیّ و دلها را توانگَر می‌کُنَند

خانه خالی کن دِلا تا مَنزلِ جانان شَوَد
کایَن هَوَسناکان دل و جان جایِ لَشکَر می‌کُنَند

صُبحدَم از عَرش می‌آمد خُروشی عَقل گُفت
قُدسیان گویی که شِعرِ حافظ از بَر می‌کُنَند

FORTY

Preachers who display their piety in prayer and pulpit
behave differently when they're alone.

I have a question! Ask the theologian among his colleagues:
"Why do those who demand repentance do so little of it?"

It's as if they don't believe in the Day of Judgment
with all this fraud and counterfeit they do in His name.

I am the slave of the tavern-master, whose dervishes,
in needing nothing, make treasure seem like dust.

O lord, put them on their old asses, the nouveaux-riches
who flaunt their mules and Turkish slaves.

O angel, say praises at the door of love's tavern
for inside they ferment the essence of Adam.

Whenever his limitless beauty kills a lover
others spring up, with love, from the invisible world.

O beggar at the cloister door, come to the monastery of the Magi,
for the water they give makes hearts rich.

Empty your house, O heart, so that it may become home to the beloved,
for the heart of the shallow ones is an army camp.

At dawn a clamor came from the throne of heaven. Reason said,
"It seems the angels are memorizing Háfiz's verse."

چهل و یک

سال‌ها دَفتَرِ ما در گِرُوِ صَهبا بود
رَونَقِ میکَدِه از دَرس و دُعای ما بود

نیکیِ پیرِ مُغان بین که چو ما بَدمَستان
هَر چه کردیم به چَشمِ کَرَمَش زیبا بود

دَفتَرِ دانِشِ ما جُمله بِشویید به می
کِه فَلَک دیدَم و در قَصدِ دِلِ دانا بود

از بُتان آن طَلَب اَر حسن شِناسی ای دل
کاین کَسی گُفت که در عِلمِ نَظَر بینا بود

دِل چو پَرگار به هَر سو دَوَرانی می‌کرد
و اَندر آن دایره سَرگَشته پابرجا بود

مُطرِب از دردِ مُحَبَّت عَمَلی می‌پَرداخت
که حَکیمانِ جَهان را مُژه خون پالا بود

می‌شِکُفتَم ز طَرَب زان که چو گُل بر لَبِ جوی
بر سَرَم سایهٔ آن سَروِ سَهی بالا بود

پیرِ گُلرَنگِ من اندر حقِ اَزرَق پوشان
رُخصَتِ خُبث نَداد اَر نه حِکایت‌ها بود

قَلبِ اَندودهٔ حافظ بَر او خَرج نشد
کاین مُعامِل به هَمه عیبِ نَهان بینا بود

FORTY-ONE

For years our book was pawned for wine.
The tavern's luster came from our lessons and prayers.

See the goodness of the Magus, for as we staggered, drunk,
his generous eye saw beauty in whatever we did.

Wash my book of knowledge clean with wine
for I have seen the world, and it lies in wait for wise me.

O heart, if you are a connoisseur of beauty, seek its essence from the idols,
for this was said by someone with expert vision.

Like a compass, the heart spun in all directions,
and bewildered, stood firmly in that circle.

The minstrel played improvisations on the pain of love
so that the wise ones of the world shed tears of blood.

Like the rose at the stream's edge I blossomed with joy
for I lay in the protective shadow of that tall cypress.

My rose-colored master would hear no malice against those blue-clad ones,
otherwise there was much to say.

Háfiz could not offer his heart to the beloved
because he was wise to every hidden fault.

چهل و دو

تا ز میخانه و می نام و نشان خواهد بود
سَرِ ما خاکِ رَهِ پیرِ مُغان خواهد بود

حَلقهٔ پیرِ مُغان از اَزَلم درگوش است
بَر همانیم که بودیم و همان خواهد بود

بَر سَرِ تُربَتِ ما چون گُذَری همّت خواه
که زیارتگَهِ رِندانِ جَهان خواهد بود

بُرو ای زاهدِ خودبین که ز چَشمِ من و تو
رازِ این پَرده نَهان است و نَهان خواهد بود

تُرکِ عاشق کُشِ من مَست بُرون رفت امروز
تا دِگر خونِ که از دیده روان خواهد بود

چَشمَم آن دَم که ز شَوقِ تو نهَد سَر به لَحَد
تا دَمِ صُبحِ قیامَت نِگران خواهد بود

بَختِ حافظ گر ازین دستِ مَدَد خواهد داد
زُلفِ معشوق به دَستِ دِگران خواهد بود

FORTY-TWO

As long as the wine and tavern exist
our head will be dust on the Magus's road.

His slave-ring has been in our ear since before creation.
As we were then, we are and will always be.

When you pass by our tomb wish for spiritual power
for to the rends of the world it will be a place of pilgrimage.

O vain ascetic, go, because from your eyes and mine
the veil's secret is hidden and will always be hidden.

My Turk, that killer of lovers, went out drunk today.
Let's see who else will feel the blood flow from his eyes.

On that night when I lay my head on my grave longing for you
my eye will peer anxiously until the dawn of Resurrection.

As long as Háfiz's luck provides this kind of help
the beloved's hair will run through the fingers of others.

چهل و سه

گر من از باغِ تو یک میوه بچینَم چه شَوَد
پیشِ پایی به چِراغِ تو ببینَم چه شَوَد

یا رَب اَندَر کَنَفِ سایهٔ آن سَروِ بُلَند
گر منِ سوخته یِک دَم بِنِشینَم چه شَوَد

آخِر ای خاتَمِ جَمشیدِ هُمایون آثار
گر فِتَد عَکسِ تو بَر نَقشِ نِگینَم چه شَوَد

واعِظِ شَهر چو مِهرِ مَلِک و شَحنه گُزید
من اگر مِهرِ نِگاری بِگُزینَم چه شَوَد

عَقلَم از خانه به دَر رفت و اگر مِی این است
دیدَم از پیش که در خانهٔ دینَم چه شَوَد

صَرف شُد عُمرِ گِرانمایه به مَعشوقه و می
تا از آنَم چه به پیش آید از اینَم چه شَوَد

خواجه دانست که من عاشقَم و هیچ نگفت
حافِظ اَر نیز بداند که چُنینَم چه شَوَد

FORTY-THREE

If I pick one fruit from your garden, what does it matter?
If I make my way by the light of your radiance, what does it matter?

O lord, if my charred self sits for one moment
in the shade of that tall cypress, what does it matter?

O seal of auspicious Jamshid, if at last your reflection
should fall on my ruby bezel, what does it matter?

The city preacher chose the affection of king and constable.
If I choose the affection of a slender beauty, what does it matter?

My reason left its house, and from what I've seen,
if this is wine's work, in the house of my faith what could happen?

I spent my precious life on the beloved and on wine.
Let's see what comes to me from the one, and from the other.

The lord knew I was in love and said nothing.
If Háfiz knows this also, what does it matter?

چهل و چهار

گفتم غمِ تو دارم گفتا غمت سر آید
گفتم که ماهِ من شو گفتا اگر برآید

گفتم ز مهر ورزان رسمِ وفا بیاموز
گفتا ز خوبرویان این کار کمتر آید

گفتم که بر خیالت راهِ نظر ببندم
گفتا که شب رو است او و از راهِ دیگر آید

گفتم که بوی زلفت گمراهِ عالم کرد
گفتا اگر بدانی هم اوت رهبر آید

گفتم خوشا هوایی کز بادِ صبح خیزد
گفتا خنک نسیمی کز کوی دلبر آید

گفتم که نوشِ لعلت ما را به آرزو کشت
گفتا تو بندگی کن کو بنده پرور آید

گفتم دلِ رحیمت کی عزمِ صلح دارد
گفتا مگوی با کس تا وقتِ آن درآید

گفتم زمانِ عشرت دیدی که چون سر آمد
گفتا خموش حافظ کاین غصه هم سر آید

FORTY-FOUR

I said, "I suffer because of you." She said, "Your suffering will end."
I said, "Become my moon." She said, "If it comes to pass."

I said, "From lovers learn the custom of loyalty."
She said, "Among moon-faced ones it is rarely found."

I said, "I will barricade your image from the road of my sight."
She said, "It is a thief, and will come by a different way."

I said, "The scent of your hair has led me astray in the world."
She said, "If you understand, it can also be your guide."

I said, "Happy is the wind that rises in the garden of beauty."
She said, "Fresh is the breeze that comes from my alleyway."

I said, "Thirst for your ruby lip killed us with longing."
She said, "Serve it, for it comes to nourish its servants."

I said, "When does your merciful heart intend a truce?"
She said, "Speak of this to no one until that time comes."

I said, "Did you see how those joyful times ended?"
She said, "Be quiet, Háfiz. This grief will also end."

چهل و پنج

شَراب و عیشِ نَهان چیست کارِ بی‌بنیاد
زدیم بَر صَفِ رِندان و هر چه بادا باد

گِره ز دل بگُشا وَز سِپهر یاد مَکن
که فِکرِ هیچ مُهَندِس چُنین گِره نگُشاد

ز انقلابِ زَمانه عَجَب مَدار که چَرخ
ازیــن فَسانه هــزاران هـزار دارد یاد

قَدَح به شَرطِ اَدَب گیر زان که تَرکیبَش
ز کاسهٔ سَرِ جَمشید و بَهمَن است و قُباد

که آگَه است که کاووس و کی کُجا رفتند
که واقِف است که چون رفت تَختِ جَم بر باد

ز حَسرتِ لَبِ شیرین هَنوز می‌بینم
که لاله می‌دَمَد از خونِ دیدهٔ فرهاد

مَگر که لاله بدانِست بی‌وفاییِ دَهر
که تا بِزاد و بِشُد جامِ می ز کف نَنهاد

بیا بیا که زَمانی ز می خَراب شویم
مَگر رسیم به گَنجی درین خَراب آباد

نمی‌دهند اجازت مَرا به سیر و سَفَر
نَسیمِ بادِ مُصَلا وُ آبِ رُکن آباد

قَدَح مَگیر چو حافظ مَگَر به نالهٔ چنگ
که بَسته‌اند بر اَبریشمِ طرَب دلِ شاد

FORTY-FIVE

It is futile to revel and drink wine in secret.
I join the circle of rends, and what will be will be.

Open the knot of your heart and give no thought to fate.
No astrologer has ever unraveled such a problem.

Don't be surprised by the ravages of time, for the turning wheel
remembers thousands upon thousands of such stories.

Grasp the cup with polite respect—it is made
from the skulls of Jamshid, Bahman, and Qobad.

Who knows where Kavus and the other kings went?
Who knows how the throne of Jamshid disappeared?

I see that, for love of Shirin's lips,
tulips still grow from the grave of Farhad.

There's no doubt the tulip understood the world's infidelity.
Between birth and death it never put down its cup.

Come, for a while let's ruin ourselves with wine.
Perhaps we will find treasure in this ruined world.

The gentle breeze of Musallah and the waters of Ruknabad
don't allow me to go anywhere else.

Like Háfiz, never take up a cup without the music of the lyre,
because a happy heart is tied to the silk strings of joy.

چهل و شش

آنکه رُخسارِ تو را رَنگِ گُل و نَسرین داد
صَبر و آرام تَواند به منِ مِسکین داد

وانکه گیسویِ تو را رَسمِ تطاوُل آموخت
هم تَواند کَرَمش داد منِ غَمگین داد

من هَمان روز ز فَرهاد طَمَع بُبریدَم
که عِنانِ دِل شیدا به لَبِ شیرین داد

گَنجِ زَر گر نَبُوَد کُنجِ قَناعَت باقیست
آن که آن داد به شاهان به گدایان این داد

خوش عَروسیست جَهان از رَه صورَت لیکن
هرکه پیوَست بدو عُمرِ خودَش کاوین داد

بعد ازین دَستِ من و دامَنِ سَرو و لَبِ جویْ
خاصه اَکنون که صبا مُژدهٔ فَرَوَردین داد

در کَفِ غُصّهٔ دوران دل حافظ خون شد
در فِراقِ رُخَت ای خواجهٔ قوام‌الدین داد

FORTY-SIX

The one who gave your face the colors of the rose and jonquil
could surely give patience and peace to wretched me

and the one who taught the curls of your hair the way of destruction,
his compassion could give justice to me, the sad one.

I gave up hope for Farhad on the day
that he gave to Shirin's lips the reins of his frenzied heart.

Although there is no treasure of gold, there is the corner of contentment.
The one who gave that to kings gave this to beggars.

In appearance, the world is a beautiful bride.
Whoever married her gave his life as his marriage-portion.

After this, there is just my hand clutching the cypress's hem on the bank
    of the stream,
especially now that the dawn wind has brought news of spring.

The hand of grief-filled time holds Háfiz's crushed and bloodied heart.
Your face is gone, O lord Qavam ud-Dín, and I cry out "Alas!"

چهل و هفت

صَبا زِ مَنزِلِ جانان گُذَر دَریغ مَدار
وَزو به عاشِقِ بی‌دِل خَبَر دَریغ مَدار

به شُکرِ آن که شِکُفتی به کام بخت ای گُل
نَسیمِ وَصل زِ مُرغِ سَحَر دَریغ مَدار

حَریفِ عشقِ تو بودَم چو ماه نو بودی
کُنون که ماه تَمامی نَظَر دَریغ مَدار

کُنون که چِشمهٔ قَند است لَعل نوشینَت
سُخَن بگوی و زِ طوطی شِکَر دَریغ مَدار

جَهان و هرچه دراو هست سَهل و مُختَصَر است
زِ اَهلِ مَعرِفَت این مُختَصَر دَریغ مَدار

مَکارِمِ تو به آفاق می‌بَرد شاعر
ازو وَظیفه و زادِ سَفَر دَریغ مَدار

چو ذِکرِ خِیر طَلَب می‌کنی سُخَن این است
که در بَهای سُخَن سیم و زر دَریغ مَدار

غُبارِ غَم بِرَوَد حال خوش شَوَد حافظ
تو آبِ دیده ازین رَهگُذَر دَریغ مَدار

FORTY-SEVEN

O gentle wind, don't refuse to pass by the house of the beloved,
and don't keep news of her from the lost-hearted lover.

O rose, you unfolded as your heart desired. In gratitude,
don't keep the wind of union from the bird of dawn.

When you were a new moon I was your love's companion.
Now that you are a full moon don't withhold your glance.

Now that your sweet ruby lip is the source of sugar,
speak, and don't keep sugar from the parrot.

This world, with all it contains, is slight and brief.
Don't keep this trifle from people of insight.

The poet carries word of your generosity to all horizons.
Don't withhold compensation and provisions for his journey.

If you want people to speak well of you, there is a saying:
"Don't refrain from giving gold and silver for fine words."

The dust of sorrow will subside. Happiness will come.
For now, Háfiz, don't keep your tears from this roadway.

چهل و هشت

اَلا ای طوطیِ گویایِ اسرار
مَبادا خالیَت شِکَّر زِ منقار

سَرَت سَبز و دِلَت خوش باد جاوید
که خوش نَقشی نِمودی از خطِ یار

سُخَن سَربَسته گُفتی با حَریفان
خدا را زین مُعَمّا پَرده بردار

بـه رویِ مـا زَن از ساغَر گُلابی
که خواب آلودهایم ای بختِ بیدار

چه ره بود این که زَد در پَردهِ مُطرب
که میرَقصَند با هَم مَست و هُشیار

ازین اَفیون که ساقی در مِی اَفکَند
حَریفان را نه سر ماند و نه دَستار

سِکَندَر را نِمیبَخشَند آبی
به زور و زَر مُیَسَّر نیست این کار

خِرَد هَرچَند نقدِ کاینات است
چه سَنجَد پیشِ عِشقِ کیمیاکار

بیـا و حـالِ اَهـلِ دَرد بِشنو
به لَفظِ اَندَک و مَعنیِّ بِسیار

بُتِ چینی عَدویِ دین و دِلهاست
خداوندا دِل و دینَم نِگَه دار

به مَستوران مَگو اَسرارِ مَستی
حدیثِ جان مَگو با نَقشِ دیوار

FORTY-EIGHT

Hey, O parrot, speaker of secrets!
May your beak never lack sugar!

May you live long, may your heart be happy forever,
for you have shown us a lovely image of the friend's figure.

You spoke in riddles with the companions.
For God's sake, lift the veil from this enigma.

O bright luck, splash our face with wine
for we are stained with sleep.

What melody did the minstrel play behind the veil
that the drunk and sober dance together?

Because the saqi laced the wine with opium
the companions lost their heads and turbans.

They kept the water of life from Alexander.
It cannot be found with force and gold.

Although reason is the currency of existence,
how can it compare to love, the work of the alchemist?

Come and listen to the state of the anguished ones
who speak with few words and much meaning.

The Chinese idol is the foe of faith and heart.
O lord, guard my heart and faith.

Don't reveal to the ascetic the secrets of drunkenness.
Don't speak words of the soul to the picture on the wall.

به یُمنِ دَولَتِ مَنصورِ شاهی عَلَم شُد حافظ اَندَر نَظمِ اَشعار

خداوَندی به جای بندگان کرد
خداوَندا ز آفاتش نِگه دار

Under the illustrious banner of Mansúr Sháh
Háfiz has become famous for the crafting of verse.

A lord did his duty on behalf of his slaves.
O lord, protect him from calamities.

چهل و نه

عید است و آخرِ گُل و یاران در انتظار
ساقی به روی شاه ببین ماه و می بیار

دل برگِرِفته بودَم از ایّامِ گُل ولی
کاری بِکَرد هِمَّتِ پاکانِ روزه‌دار

دل در جهان مَبَند و زِ مَستی سؤال کُن
از فیضِ جام و قِصّهٔ جَمشیدِ کامکار

جُز نَقدِ جان به دَست نَدارم شراب کو
کان نیز بر کِرِشمهٔ ساقی کُنَم نثار

گر فَوت شُد سَحور چه نُقصان صَبوح هست
از می کُنَند روزه گُشا طالِبانِ یار

تَرسَم که روزِ حَشر عِنان بر عِنان رَوَد
تَسبیحِ شیخ و خِرقهٔ رِندِ شَرابخوار

خوش دَولَتیست خُرَّم و خوش خُسرُوی کَریم
یا رَب زِ چَشمِ‌زَخمِ زَمانَش نگاه دار

می خور به شِعرِ بَنده که زیبی دِگر دهَد
جامِ مُرَصَّعِ تو بِدین دُرِّ شاهوار

زان جا که پَردِه پوشی عَفوِ کَریم توست
بر قَلبِ ما بِبَخش که نَقدیست کَم‌عیار

حافظ چو رفت روزه و گُل نیز می‌رَوَد
ناچار بادِه نوش که از دست رفت کار

FORTY-NINE

It's *'íd*, here is the last of the roses, and the friends are waiting.
Saqi, see the new moon in the friend's face, and bring wine.

My heart had given up on the time of the roses but
the will of the pure fast-keepers has worked wonders.

Don't tie your heart to the world, and ask a drunk
about the cup's bounty and the story of prosperous Jamshid.

My hand holds nothing but the coins of my soul. Where is the wine?
So that I can scatter them, too, after the saqi's glance.

If *sahúr* has passed, so what? We have the morning cup.
Those who seek the friend break their fast with wine.

I fear that the shaikh's rosary and the coat of the wine-drinking *rend*
will run neck and neck on Resurrection Day.

It is a happy time. We have a kind and generous king.
O God, protect him from time's evil eye.

Drink wine as you listen to my verse, for your jeweled cup
will give to this royal pearl a different beauty.

To overlook is the essence of your generous forgiveness.
Forgive our heart, which is a coin of few carats.

Háfiz, since the fast has gone and the rose will also go,
you can only drink wine. It's out of your hands.

پنجاه

ای صبا نکهتی از خاک رهِ یار بیار
ببر اندوهِ دل و مژدهٔ دلدار بیار

نکته‌ای روح فزا از دهنِ دوست بگو
نامه‌ای خوش خبر از عالمِ اسرار بیار

تا معطّر کنم از لطفِ نسیم تو مشام
شمّه‌ای از نفحاتِ نفسِ یار بیار

به وفای تو که خاکِ رهِ آن یارِ عزیز
بی‌غباری که پدید آید از اغیار بیار

گردی از رهگذرِ دوست به کوریِ رقیب
بهرِ آسایشِ این دیدهٔ خونبار بیار

خامی و ساده دلی شیوهٔ جانبازان نیست
خبری از برِ آن دلبرِ عیّار بیار

شکرِ آن را که تو در عشرتی ای مرغِ چمن
به اسیرانِ قفس مژدهٔ گلزار بیار

کامِ جان تلخ شد از صبر که کردم بی دوست
عشوه‌ای زان لبِ شیرینِ شکربار بیار

روزگاریست که دل چهرهٔ مقصود ندید
ساقیا آن قدحِ آینه کردار بیار

دلقِ حافظ به چه ارزد به می‌اش رنگین کن
وانگهش مست و خراب از سرِ بازار بیار

FIFTY

O dawn wind, bring the scent of dust from the friend's road.
Take grief from my heart and bring good news of her.

Repeat for me an uplifting witticism from her mouth.
Bring a letter of good news from the world of secrets.

To perfume my nose, let your gentle breeze
bring a bit of scent from her breath.

On your loyalty, bring dust from that dear love's road,
free of the dust stirred up by strangers.

In spite of her guardian, bring dust from her road.
With that kohl I can soothe these eyes that rain blood.

Naivete and a simple heart aren't for those who would give up their life.
Bring me news of that savvy young thing.

O bird of the field, we rejoice that you live in pleasure.
To the cage's captives bring glad tidings from the garden.

The soul's mouth grew bitter from waiting without her.
Bring a sultry gesture from those lips that scatter sugar.

For a long time my heart did not see the face it sought.
O saqi, bring that mirror-like cup.

What's the coat of Háfiz worth? Stain it with wine,
then bring him, drunk and ruined, from the heart of the bazaar.

پنجاه و یک

روی بِنمای و وُجودِ خُودَم از یاد بِبَر
خَرمَنِ سوختِگان را هَمـه گو باد بِبَر

ما چو دادیم دِل و دیدِه به طوفانِ بَلا
گو بیا سِیلِ غَم و خانـه زِ بُنیاد بِبَر

زُلفِ چون عَنبَرِ خامَش که بِبویَد هیهات
ای دِلِ خام طَمَع این سُخَن از یاد بِبَر

سینـه گو شُعلـهٔ آتَشکَدهٔ فارِس بِکُش
دیده گو آبِ رُخِ دَجلـهٔ بَغداد بِبَر

سـعی نـابُردِه در این راه به جایی نَرسی
مُزد اگر مـیطَلَبی طاعَتِ اُستاد بِبَر

دَولَتِ پیرِ مُغان باد که باقی سَهل است
دیگری گو بُرو وُ نامِ من از یاد بِبَر

روزِ مَرگَم نَفَسی وَعدهٔ دیدار بِده
وانگَهَم تا بِه لَحَد فارِغ و آزاد بِبَر

دوش مـیگفت به مـژگانِ درازَت بِکُشَم
یا رَب از خاطِرَش اندیشهٔ بیداد بِبَر

حافِظ اَندیشـه کُن از نازُکیِ خاطِرِ یار
بُرو از دَرگَهَش این نالـه وُ فَریاد بِبَر

FIFTY-ONE

Show your face and make me forget I exist.
And the pile of burned ones, tell the wind to take them.

Since we gave up our heart and eyes to the storm of affliction
say, "Come, flood of sorrow, tear this house from its foundations."

Who can possibly smell the fresh ambergris of her curls?
O unripe and greedy heart, forget this matter!

You could say that my breast overwhelms the fire-temple of Fars.
You could say that my eyes disgrace the Tigris of Baghdad.

Without effort on this road you will go nowhere.
If you seek the reward, do the will of your teacher.

Long live the Magus, for the rest is nothing.
To anyone else say, "Go, and forget my name."

Let me see you for one moment on the day of my death
and then take me, unfettered and free, to my grave.

Last night she said, "I will kill you with my long eyelashes."
O lord, banish the thought of injustice from her mind.

Háfiz, consider the beloved's sensitive nature.
Leave her threshold. Take this whining and wailing with you.

پنجاه و دو

بیا و کشتیِ ما در شطِ شراب انداز
خروش و ولوله در جانِ شیخ و شاب انداز

مرا به کشتیِ باده درافکن ای ساقی
که گفته‌اند نکویی کن و در آب انداز

ز کویِ میکده برگشته‌ام ز راهِ خطا
مرا دِگر ز کرم با رَهِ صَواب انداز

بیار زان میِ گُلرنگِ مُشک بو جامی
شرارِ رشک و حسد در دلِ گلاب انداز

اگر چه مست و خرابم تو نیز لطفی کن
نظر بر این دلِ سرگشتهٔ خراب انداز

به نیمِ شب اگرت آفتاب می‌باید
ز رویِ دخترِ گلچهرِ رَز نقاب انداز

مَهِل که روزِ وفاتم به خاک بسپارند
مرا به میکده بر در خُمِ شراب انداز

ز جورِ چرخ چو حافظ به جان رسید دلت
به سویِ دیوِ مِحَن ناوکِ شهاب انداز

FIFTY-TWO

Come, launch my vessel into the river of wine.
Cast shouting and uproar into the souls of old and young.

Launch me into the vessel of wine, O saqi, for as they say,
"Cast your good deed out onto the waters."

I left the alley of the taverns by mistake.
Out of compassion, set me back on the right road.

Bring me a cup of that red, musk-scented wine
and strike envy and jealousy into the rose-water's heart.

Although I am drunk, completely drunk, be kind:
cast a glance at this confused and ruined heart.

If you must have the sun at midnight, pull the veil
from the face of the grape's rosy-cheeked daughter.

On the day of my death don't let them bury me.
Take me to the tavern and throw me into a cask.

Ground beneath the great wheel, your heart, like Háfiz's, has had enough.
Fire a meteor arrow at the demon of affliction.

پنجاه و سه

خیز و در کاسهٔ زر آبِ طَرَبناک انداز
پیشتر زان که شَوَد کاسهٔ سَر خاک انداز

عاقِبَت مَنزلِ ما وادیِ خاموشان است
حالیا غُلغُله در گُنبَدِ اَفلاک انداز

چَشمِ آلوده نَظَر از رُخِ جانان دور است
بَر رُخِ او نَظَر از آینهٔ پاک انداز

به سَرِ سَبزِ تو ای سَرو که گَر خاک شَوَم
ناز از سَر بِنه و سایه بَرین خاک انداز

دلِ ما را که ز مارِ سَرِ زُلفِ تو بِخَست
از لَبِ خود به شَفاخانهٔ تَریاک انداز

مِلکِ این مَزرَعه دانی که ثُباتی نَدهَد
اَتشــی از جِگَرِ جام در اَمــلاک انداز

غُسل در اَشک زَدَم کاهلِ طَریقَت گویند
پاک شَو اوّل و پَس دیده بر آن پاک انداز

یا رَب آن زاهدِ خودبین که به جُز عیب نَدید
دودِ آهـیش در آیینهٔ اِدراک انداز

چون گُل از نکهَتِ او جامه قَبا کُن حافظ
وین قَبا در رَهِ آن قامَتِ چالاک انداز

FIFTY-THREE

Get up and pour liquid joy into this gold cup.
Pour it now, before our skulls turn to dust.

At the end we will live in the valley of the silent.
Now, while you can, revel under the dome of heaven.

To look at the beloved's face with an unclean eye is not proper.
Look at her face with the pure polished mirror of your eye.

By your happy green head, O cypress, when I am dust
put coquetry aside and cast your shade over my grave.

My heart has been bitten by the snake-ends of your dark hair.
Cure it with your lips.

You know that the reign of this world will not last.
From the heart of the cup throw fire into heaven.

I made my ablutions in the pool of my tears because the path-travelers say,
"First become pure yourself, then cast a look at the pure one."

That vain ascetic who sees nothing but himself and the evil in others,
O lord, cloud the mirror of his understanding with a sigh.

Háfiz, like a rose rip your shirt at the scent of that agile one
and throw it into the road at her feet.

پنجاه و چهار

گل‌عُذاری ز گُلستانِ جَهانِ ما را بَس
زین چَمَن سایهٔ آن سَروِ رَوانِ ما را بَس

من و هم صُحبَتیِ اَهلِ ریا دورَم باد
از گِرانانِ جَهان رَطلِ گِرانِ ما را بَس

قَصرِ فِردَوس به پاداشِ عَمَل می‌بَخشَند
ما که رِندیم و گِدا دیرِ مُغانِ ما را بَس

بِنشین بَر لَبِ جوی و گُذَرِ عُمر بِبین
کاین اِشارَت ز جَهانِ گُذَرانِ ما را بَس

نَقدِ بازارِ جَهان بِنگَر و آزارِ جَهان
گر شَما را نه بَس این سود و زیانِ ما را بَس

یار با ماست چه حاجَت که زیادَت طَلَبیم
دَولَتِ صُحبَتِ آن مونِسِ جانِ ما را بَس

از دَرِ خویش خُدا را به بِهشتم مَفرِست
که سَرِ کویِ تو از کَون و مَکانِ ما را بَس

حافظ از مَشرَبِ قِسمَت گِله ناانصافیست
طَبعِ چون آب و غَزَل‌هایِ رَوانِ ما را بَس

FIFTY-FOUR

A rose-faced one from the world's garden is enough for me.
In the field, the shade of that flowing cypress is enough for me.

May I never be intimate with hypocrites.
Of the world's weighty things, a heavy cup is enough for me.

For good deeds they grant you the palace of paradise.
We rends and paupers, the Magi's cloister is enough for us.

Sit by the stream's edge and watch life pass by.
This sign from a passing world is enough for me.

See the cash in the world's bazaar, and the world's torments.
If not enough for you, this profit and loss is enough for me.

The friend is with me. Why would I look further?
Intimacy with that soul-companion is enough for me.

I am here at your door, for God's sake don't send me to heaven,
for in all the universe your narrow alleyway is enough for me.

Háfiz, it is unjust to complain about the wellspring of your fate.
A nature like water and flowing ghazals are enough for us.

پنجاه و پنج

دارم از زُلفِ سیاهَش گِله چَندان که مَپُرس
که چنان زو شُدِه‌ام بی سَر و سامان که مَپُرس

کَس به اُمّیدِ وَفا تَرکِ دل و دین مَکُناد
که چنانم من ازین کَرده پشیمان که مَپُرس

به یِکی جُرعه که آزارِ کَسَش در پی نیست
زَحمَتی می‌کِشَم از مَردُمِ نادان که مَپُرس

زاهِد از ما به سَلامَت بِگُذَر کاین می لَعل
دل و دین می‌بَرَد از دَست بدان سان که مَپُرس

پارسایی و سَلامَت هَوَسَم بود وَلی
شیوه‌ای می‌کُنَد آن نَرگِسِ فَتّان که مَپُرس

گفتگوهاست درین راه که جان بُگدازَد
هَر کَسی عَربَده‌ای این که مَبین آن که مَپُرس

گُفتَم از گویِ فَلَک صورَتِ حالی پُرسَم
گفت آن می‌کِشَم اندَر خَمِ چَوگان که مَپُرس

گُفتَمَش زُلف به خونِ که شِکَستی گفتا
حافظ این قِصّه دراز اَست به قُرآن که مَپُرس

FIFTY-FIVE

Don't ask how many complaints I have about her black hair,
for I became so undone because of her it's beyond telling.

Let no one abandon heart and faith in hope of fidelity.
I did this. Don't ask me how sorry I am.

With one innocent drink that hurt no one
I drew such trouble from the ignorant that it's beyond telling.

Ascetic, pass by. Peace be with you.
Don't ask how this ruby wine steals my heart and faith.

I desired a life of seclusion and righteousness but
the wink of that narcissus is so artful it's beyond telling.

On this road there are disputes that melt the soul.
Each one says loudly, "Don't look at this! Don't ask about that!"

I thought I would ask the orb of heaven how it was with him.
He said, "I suffer so much in the mallet's curve it's beyond telling."

I said to her, "Whose blood did you spill with your curls?"
She said, "Háfiz, it's a long story. By the Qur'an, don't ask."

پنجاه و شش

سَحَر ز هاتِفِ غِیبَم رسید مُژده به گوش
که دَورِ شاه شُجاع است می دِلیر بِنوش

شُد آن که اَهلِ نَظَر بَر کِناره می‌رفتند
هِزار گونه سُخَن در دَهان و لَب خاموش

به صوتِ چَنگ بگوییم آن حِکایَت‌ها
که از نَهُفتنِ آن دیگِ سینه می‌زد جوش

شَرابِ خانِگیِ تَرسِ مُحتَسِب خورده
به رویِ یار بِنوشیم و بانگِ نوشانوش

ز کویِ میکده دوشَش به دوش می‌بُردَند
اِمامِ شَهر که سَجّاده می‌کِشید به دوش

دِلا دِلالَتِ خِیرَت کُنَم به راهِ نِجات
مَکُن به فِسق مُباهات و زُهد هَم مَفُروش

مَحَلِّ نورِ تَجلّی‌ست رایِ اَنوَرِ شاه
چو قُربِ او طَلَبی در صَفایِ نیَّت کوش

به جُز ثَنایِ جَلالَش مَساز وِردِ ضَمیر
که هَست گوشِ دِلَش مَحرَمِ پَیامِ سُروش

رُموزِ مَصلَحَتِ مُلکِ خُسرُوان دانَند
گِدایِ گوشه نِشینی تو حافظا مَخروش

FIFTY-SIX

At dawn I heard the news from the invisible angel:
"It is the reign of Sháh Shojá'! Drink without fear!"

Gone is the time when people of insight, with so much to say,
walked at the margins in silence.

To the sound of the lyre we will sing the hidden stories
that have been boiling in the cauldron of our breast.

We will drink that home-made wine, aged in fear of the *muhtasib*,
and to the friend's health and shout "*Núshanúsh!*"

Last night, from the alley of the taverns,
they even carried home our pious lord imam.

O heart, let me guide you to the path of salvation:
don't boast of debauchery or pretend to be pious.

God's light shines in the mind of the king.
If you want to be near him, try to be pure.

Keep nothing in your heart but praise for his grandeur
for the ear of his heart is attuned to the angel's voice.

Kings know what's best for their realm.
You, Háfiz, are a beggar in the corner. Be quiet.

پنجاه و هفت

دوش بـا مـن گُفت پنهـان کاردانـی تیزهـوش
کَز شُمـا پنهـان نَشـایَد کَرد سِـرِّ مِـی فروش

گُفت آسـان گیر بر خود کارها کَز روی طَبـع
سَخت مـی‌گیرد جَهان بـر مَردُمـانِ سَخت کـوش

وانگَهَـم دَر داد جـامی کَز فُروغَـش بَر فَلَک
زُهـره در رَقص آمَـد و بَربَط زَنـان می‌گُفت نـوش

بـا دلِ خـونیـن لبِ خَنـدان بیـاوَر هَمچـو جـام
نـی گَرَت زَخمی رِسَد آیی چـو چَنگ اَندَر خُروش

تا نَگَردی آشنـا زیـن پَرده رَمـزی نشنـوی
گوشِ نـامَحرَم نَبـاشَد جـای پِیغـامِ سُروش

گوش کُـن پَند ای پسَر وَز بَهر دُنیا غَـم مَخور
گُفتَمَت چـون دُرّ حَدیثی گَر تَوانـی داشت هـوش

در حَریمِ عشـق نَتوان زَد دَم از گُفت و شنیـد
زان که آنجـا جُملهِ اَعضا چَشم بـاید بـود و گـوش

بَر بَساطِ نُکتـه دانـان خودفُروشـی شَرط نیست
یا سُخَن دانِستـه گو ای مَردِ عـاقِل یا خَمـوش

ساقیـا مـی ده کـه رندی‌هـای حافظ فَهم کرد
آصِـفِ صـاحِب قَـرانِ جُرم بَخشِ عِیب پوش

FIFTY-SEVEN

Last night a wise, keen-minded one whispered to me,
"The wine-seller's secret should not be hidden from you."

He said, "Take it easy, for by its nature
the world is hard on those who try hard."

And then he gave me a cup, and in its light, across the heavens,
Venus began to dance, and played her lute, and cried, "Drink!"

While your heart bleeds let your lips smile like the cup.
If you are struck, don't break into a roar like the harp.

Until you are an initiate, you will not hear a secret in this music.
The outsider's ear is no place for the angel's message.

Listen to my advice, O son, and don't worry about the world.
I gave you a pearl of advice, if you can hear it.

In love's sanctuary there is no bickering back and forth
because there all your limbs must be eye and ear.

In the shop of those who understand subtlety, hawking oneself
is not allowed. Speak thoughtfully, O wise one, or be quiet.

O saqi, give us wine, because the Ásaf of our time,
forgiver of sins and overlooker of faults, understands what Háfiz really means.

پنجاه و هشت

هِزار دُشمَنَم اَر می‌کُنَند قَصدِ هَلاك
گَرَم تو دوستی از دُشمَنان نَدارم باك

مَرا اُمیدِ وِصالِ تو زِنده می‌دارَد
وَ گَر نَه هر دَمَم از هِجرِ توست بیمِ هَلاك

نَفَس نَفَس اَگر اَز باد نَشنَوَم بویَش
زَمان زَمان چو گُل از غَم کُنَم گَریبان چاك

رَوَد بـه خواب دو چَشم از خیالِ تو هیهات
بُوَد صَبور دل اَندَر فِراقِ تو حاشاك

اَگَر تو زَخم زَنی بِه که دیگَری مَرهَم
وَگَر تو زَهر دَهی بِه که دیگَری تریاك

بِضَربِ سَیفِکَ قَتلی حَیاتُنا اَبَداً
لاَنَّ روحیَ قَد طابَ اَن یَکُونَ فِداك

عِنان مَپیچ که گَر می‌زَنی بِه شَمشیرَم
سِپَرکُنَم سَر و دَستَت نَدارم از فِتراك

تو را چنان که تویی هَر نَظَر کُجا بیند
بِه قَدرِ دانِشِ خود هَر کَسی کُنَد ادراك

بِه چَشمِ خَلق عَزیز آن زَمان شَوَد حافظ
که بَر دَرِ تو نَهَد روی مَسکَنَت بَر خاك

FIFTY-EIGHT

If thousands of my enemies set out to destroy me
I have nothing to fear if you are my friend.

Hope for union with you keeps me alive,
otherwise, far from you, every moment I would fear death.

If I don't smell your scent on the wind with every breath
then every time, like the rose, in sorrow I will tear my shirt.

Could eyes close in sleep, thinking of you? Alas, no.
Could the heart be patient, separated from you? Never.

A heart-wound from you is better than the salve of another.
Poison from you is better than the antidote of another.

Death by your sword grants me eternal life
because my soul will rejoice in its sacrifice.

If you ride at me with your sword, don't turn the horse aside.
I will offer the shield of my head and will never let go of your saddle.

Can any eye see you as you are?
Each of us sees you as best we can.

The people will look up to Háfiz
when he buries the face of destitution in the dust of your doorway.

پنجاه و نه

فاش می‌گویَم و از گُفتهٔ خود دلشادَم
بَندهٔ عِشقَم و از هَر دو جَهان آزادَم

طایرِ گُلشَنِ قُدسَم چِه دِهَم شَرحِ فِراق
که دَرین دامگَهِ حادِثه چون اُفتادَم

مَن مَلَک بودَم و فِردَوسِ بَرین جایَم بود
آدَم آوَرد دَرین دِیرِ خَراب آبادَم

سایهٔ طوبی و دِلجویی حور و لَبِ حَوض
به هَوای سَرِ کوی تو بِرَفت از یادَم

نیست بَر لَوحِ دِلَم جُزِ اَلِفِ قامَتِ دوست
چِه کُنَم حَرفِ دِگَر یاد نَداد اُستادَم

کَوکَبِ بَختِ مَرا هیچ مُنَجِّم نَشناخت
یا رَب از مادَرِ گیتی به چِه طالِع زادَم

تا شُدَم حَلقه به گوشِ دَرِ میخانهٔ عِشق
هَر دَم آیَد غَمی از نَو به مُبارک بادَم

می‌خورَد خونِ دِلَم مَردُمَکِ دیده سِزاست
که چِرا دِل به جِگَرگوشهٔ مَردُم دادَم

پاک کُن چِهرهٔ حافظ به سَرِ زُلف ز اَشک
وَرنه این سِیلِ دَمادَم بِبَرَد بُنیادَم

FIFTY-NINE

I speak frankly and that makes me happy.
I am the slave of love. I am free of both worlds.

I am a bird of heaven's garden. How do I describe the pain of separation,
my fall into this snare of the world?

I was an angel and highest paradise was my place.
Adam brought me to this monastery in the city of ruin.

The houris' caress, the pool and shade trees of paradise
were forgotten in the breeze from your alleyway.

There is nothing on the tablet of my heart but my love's tall *alif*.
What can I do? My master taught me no other letter.

No astrologer knew the constellations of my fate.
O lord, when I was born of mother earth which stars were rising?

Ever since I became a slave at the door of love's tavern
sorrows come to me each moment with congratulations.

The pupil of my eye drains the blood from my heart.
I deserve it. Why did I give my heart to the darling of others?

Wipe the tears from Háfiz's face with soft curls
or else this endless torrent will uproot me.

شصت

مُژدهٔ وَصلِ تو کو کز سَرِ جان بَرخیزم
طایرِ قُدسَم و از دامِ جَهان بَرخیزم

بِه وَلای تو که گر بَندهٔ خویشَم خوانی
از سَرِ خواجِگیِ کَون و مَکان بَرخیزم

یا رَب از ابرِ هِدایَت بِرسان بارانی
پیشتَر زان که چو گَردی ز میان بَرخیزم

بَر سَرِ تُربَتِ مَن با می و مُطرِب بِنشین
تا به بویَت ز لَحَد رَقص کُنان بَرخیزم

گر چه پیرَم تو شَبی تَنگ دَر آغوشَم کَش
تا سَحَرگَه ز کِنارِ تو جَوان بَرخیزم

خیز و بالا بِنما ای بُتِ شیرین حَرَکات
تا چو حافظ ز سَرِ جان و جَهان بَرخیزم

SIXTY

Where is the good news of union with you, so I can give up my life?
I am a bird of paradise and will escape the snare of this world.

On your love I swear: call me your slave
and I will give up the crown of the whole universe.

O lord, send a little rain from that nurturing cloud
before I am blown away like a speck of dust.

Come and sit by my tomb with wine and music
because your presence will make me rise up and dance.

Although I am old, for just one night hold me
so that at dawn I will rise up from your side a young man.

Rise up and reveal your true stature, O sweet dancing idol,
and, like Háfiz, I will give up this world and my life.

شصت و یک

حِجابِ چِهرهٔ جان می‌شَوَد غُبارِ تَنَم
خوشا دَمی که از آن چِهره پَرده بَرفِکَنَم

چُنین قَفَس نه سزای چو مَن خوش اَلحانی‌ست
رَوَم به گلشَن رِضوان که مُرغِ آن چَمَنَم

عَیان نَشُد که چِرا آمَدَم کُجا بودَم
دَریغ و دَرد که غافِل ز کارِ خویشتَنَم

چِگونه طَوف کُنَم در فَضایِ عالَم قُدس
چو دَر سَراچهٔ ترکیبِ تَختِه بَندِ تَنَم

اگر ز خونِ دِلَم بوی شُوقِ می‌آید
عَجَب مَدار که هَمدَردِ نافهٔ خُتَّنَم

طَرازِ پیرهَنِ زَرکِشَم مَبین چون شَمع
که سوزهاست نَهانی دَرونِ پیرهَنَم

بیا و هَستی حافظ ز پیشِ او بَردار
که با وجودِ تو کَس نَشنَوَد ز مَن که مَنَم

SIXTY-ONE

The dust of my body veils the face of my soul.
Happy the moment I can pull the veil from that face.

To be caged is unjust, because my voice is beautiful.
I am a bird of heaven's garden. I will go there.

Where I was and why I came isn't clear.
I hurt and suffer because I don't understand.

How can I wander through the vast expanse of heaven
when I am boarded up in the mud brick house of my body?

If the scent of joy spills from my heart's blood, don't be surprised,
for I am in the same pain as the musk-deer of Khotan.

Don't be distracted by the flickering of my gold-embroidered shirt,
for, as with the candle, a burning hides beneath it.

Come, take Háfiz's existence from him.
As long as there is you no one will hear from me that I am I.

شصت و دو

در خَرابـاتِ مُـغان نـورِ خُدا مـی‌بیـنَم
این عَجَب بین که چهِ نوری زِ کُجا می‌بینَم

جِلوِه بَر من مَفُروش ای مَلِکُ الحاج که تو
خانه مـی‌بینی و مَن خانـه خُدا می‌بینَم

خواهَم از زُلفِ بُتـان نافِه گُشایـی کَردَن
فِکر دور است هَمـانا که خَطا می‌بینَم

سـوزِ دِل اَشـکِ رَوان آه سـحر نالهٔ شب
ایـن هَمـه از نَظَـرِ لُطفِ شُما می‌بینَم

هَردَم از روی تو نَقشی زَنَدَم راهِ خیـال
بـا که گویَم که در این پَردِه چه‌ها مـی‌بینَم

کس ندیده‌ست زِ مُشکِ خُتَن و نافهٔ چین
آنچِه مـن از هَر سَحَر از بادِ صَبا مـی‌بینَم

دوستـان عیب نَظَربازی حافظ مَکُنید
که مـن او را زِ مُحِبّـانِ خُدا مـی‌بینَم

SIXTY-TWO

In the Magi's tavern I see the light of God.
How strange to see such a light in such a place.

O leader of the Hajj caravan, don't show off to me.
You will see the house of the lord but here I see the lord of the house.

I want to unlock the scent of the idols' musky dark curls
but this is wishful thinking, and beyond me.

A burning heart. Flowing tears. The cry at night. The sigh at dawn.
Because of your kindness, all these are mine.

Each moment my mind creates a new image of your face.
Who can I tell of the wonders I see on this screen?

No one has ever smelled, in the musk of Khotan or China,
the scent the dawn wind brings to me every morning.

Friends, don't fault Háfiz for his flirtatious glances
because I know him as one who loves God.

شصت و سه

خُرَّم آن روز کَزین مَنزِلِ ویران بِرَوَم
راحَتِ جان طَلَبَم وَز پِی جانان بِرَوَم

گَرچِه دانَم که به جایی نَبَرَد راه غَریب
مَن به بویِ سَرِ آن زُلفِ پَریشان بِرَوَم

چون صَبا با تَنِ بیمار و دِلِ بی‌طاقَت
به هَواداریِ آن سَروِ خَرامان بِرَوَم

دِلَم از وَحشَتِ زِندانِ سِکَندَر بِگِرِفت
رَخت بَربَندَم و تا مُلکِ سُلیمان بِرَوَم

دَر رَهِ او چو قَلَم گَر به سَرَم بایَد رَفت
با دِلِ زَخم کِش و دیدهٔ گِریان بِرَوَم

نَذر کَردَم گَر ازین غَم به دَرآیَم روزی
تا دَرِ میکَده شادان و غَزَل‌خوان بِرَوَم

به هَواداریِ او ذَرّه صِفَت رَقص کُنان
تا لَبِ چِشمهٔ خورشیدِ دِرَخشان بِرَوَم

تازیان را غَمِ اَحوالِ گِرانباران نیست
پارسایان مَدَدی تا خوش و آسان بِرَوَم

وَر چو حافِظ نَبَرَم رَه ز بیابان بیرون
هَمرَهِ کوکبهٔ آصِفِ دوران بِرَوَم

SIXTY-THREE

Happy that day that I leave this ruined house.
I seek rest for my soul. I will go after the beloved.

Although I know that the stranger's road leads nowhere
I will follow the scent of his tousled curls.

Even with sick heart and failing body, like the dawn wind
I will go on adoring that striding cypress.

My heart grew weary in the isolation of Alexander's prison.
I will pack my things. I will go to the kingdom of Solomon.

Even if I must eagerly travel his road, like a pen
I will go with a weeping eye and wounded heart.

I vowed that if I emerge from this sorrow one day
I will go merrily to the tavern door, joyful and singing ghazals.

Adoring him, dancing like a dust mote,
I will go to the edge of the sun's blazing source.

Nimble riders don't feel the pain of the heavily-burdened.
Saintly ones, help me go with ease and happiness.

And if, like Háfiz, I don't find my way out of the wilderness
I will travel in the train of the Ásaf of our time.

شصت و چهار

فَتوی پیرِ مُغان دارَم و قَولیست قَدیم
که حَرام است می آنجا که نه یار است نَدیم

چاك خواهم زَدَن این دَلقِ ریایی چه کُنَم
روح را صُحبَتِ ناجِنس عَذابیست اَلیم

تا مَگَر جُرعِه فِشانَد لَبِ جانان بَر من
سالها تا شده‌ام بَر دَرِ میخانه مُقیم

مَگَرَش خِدمَتِ دیرینِ من از یاد بِرَفت
ای نَسیمِ سَحَری یاد دِهَش عَهدِ قَدیم

بَعدِ صَد سال اگر بَر سَرِ خاکَم گُذَری
سَر بَرآرَد زِ گِلَم رَقص کُنان عَظمِ رَمیم

دِلبَر از ما به صَد اُمّید سِتَد دِل اَوّل
ظاهِراً عَهد فَرامُش نَکُنَد خُلقِ کَریم

غُنچِه گو تَنگ دِل از کارِ فُروبَسته مَباش
کز دَمِ صُبح مَدَد یابی و اَنفاسِ نَسیم

فِکرِ بِهبودِ خود ای دِل زِ دَری دیگَر کُن
دَردِ عاشِق نَشَوَد بِه بِه مُداوایِ حَکیم

گوهَرِ مَعرِفَت اَندوز که با خود بِبَری
که نَصیبِ دِگَران است نِصابِ زَر و سیم

دام سَخت است مَگَر یار شَوَد لُطفِ خُدا
وَر نَه آدَم نَبَرد صَرفِه ز شِیطانِ رَجیم

حافظ اَر سیم و زَرَت نیست چه شُد شاکِر باش
چه بِه از دَولَتِ لُطفِ سُخَن و طَبعِ سَلیم

SIXTY-FOUR

I have the judgment of the Magus and it is an old saying:
"Wine is forbidden unless the friend is your companion."

I want to tear this coat of hypocrisy. What can I do?
Intimacy with unworthy people is torture to the soul.

On the chance that her lip might sprinkle me with wine
I have lived for years in the tavern doorway.

Has she forgotten my ancient service? O wind of dawn,
remind her of those days, and of her promise.

If, in a hundred years, you pass by my grave,
my rotted bones will rise up from the mud, dancing.

At the beginning she stole our heart with a hundred hopes.
Usually generous people do not forget a promise.

Say to the rosebud, "Don't despair that you are tightly folded,
for the dawn wind's breath will help bring you to life."

O heart, ponder your health at another doorway,
the lover's sickness will not improve in a physician's care.

Gather up the jewel of gnosis to carry it with you,
for wealth in gold and silver is the lot of others.

The snare is strong unless God's grace befriends you.
Otherwise what advantage did Adam have over Satan?

Háfiz, you lack silver and gold. So what? Be thankful.
What can surpass the blessings of flawless talent and exquisite verse?

شصت و پنج

ما ز یاران چَشمِ یاری داشتیم
خود غَلَط بود آن چِه می‌پِنداشتیم

تا دِرَختِ دوستی کِی بَر دِهَد
حالیا رَفتیم و تُخمی کاشتیم

گُفت و گو آیینِ دَرویشی نَبود
وَر نَه با تو ماجَراها داشتیم

شیوهٔ چَشمَت فَریبِ جَنگ داشت
ما غَلَط کَردیم و صُلح انگاشتیم

گُلبنِ حُسنَت نَه خود شُد دِلفُروز
ما دَمِ هِمَّت بَرو بُگماشتیم

نُکته‌ها رَفت و شِکایَت کَس نَکرد
جانِبِ حُرمَت فُرو نَگذاشتیم

گُفت خود دادی به ما دل حافظا
ما مُحَصِّل بَر کَسی نَگماشتیم

SIXTY-FIVE

I expected friendship from friends but
whatever I thought, it was wrong.

Who knows when the tree of friendship will bear fruit?
For now, all I can do is plant a seed.

Arguing is not a dervish tradition, otherwise
there would have been much trouble between us.

Your glance hid your intent to go to war.
I was wrong, I thought it meant peace.

The rosebush of your beauty didn't become so lovely on its own.
I nourished it with the efforts of my heart.

Despite what happened you heard no complaint.
I never relinquished my respect for you.

He said, "Háfiz, you yourself gave me your heart.
We never sent a collector to ask for it."

شصت و شش

سَرَم خوش است و به بانگِ بُلَند می‌گویَم
که من نَسیمِ حَیات از پیاله می‌بویَم

عَبوسِ زُهد به وَجهِ خُمار نَنشیند
مُریدِ خِرقهٔ دُردی کِشانِ خوش خویَم

گَرَم نه پیرِ مُغان در به روی بُگشایَد
کُدام دَر بِزَنَم چاره از کُجا جویَم

مَکُن دَرین چَمَنَم سَرزَنِش به خودرویی
چُنانکِه پَرورِشَم می‌دَهَند می‌رویَم

تو خانقاه و خَرابات دَر میانه مَبین
خُدا گَواه که هَر جا که هست با اویَم

غُبارِ راهِ طَلَب کیمیایِ بِهروزیست
غُلامِ دَولَتِ آن خاکِ عَنبَرین بویَم

زِ شَوقِ نَرگِسِ مَستِ بُلَند بالایی
چو لاله با قَدَح افتاده بَر لَبِ جویَم

شُدَم فَسانه به سَرگَشتِگیّ و گیسویِ دوست
کِشید در خَمِ چَوگانِ خویش چون گویَم

بیار می که به فَتوایِ حافظ از دلِ پاک
غُبارِ زَرق به فِیضِ قَدَح فُروشویَم

SIXTY-SIX

I am slightly drunk and loudly declare
that from the cup I smell the breeze of life.

Grim asceticism doesn't fit a tipsy face.
I am a servant of the order of the merry dreg-drinkers.

If the elder of the Magi won't open his door to me
at what door should I knock to find relief?

In this field, don't criticize me for growing wild
for as I am nourished, so I grow.

Don't make a distinction between the *khánegháh* and the tavern.
As God is my witness, wherever he is I am with him.

The dust of the seeker's road is the elixir of salvation.
I am the slave of the richness of that musk-scented dust.

Filled with the joy of my tall one's drunken eyes
like a tulip I lie with a cup on the bank of the stream.

The curl of her hair held me like a polo ball in its curve.
After that I became famous for wandering.

Bring wine, so that with a *fatwa'* from Háfiz's pure heart
by the cup's grace we can wash away the dust of hypocrisy.

شصت و هفت

بارها گفته‌ام و بارِ دِگر می‌گویم
که منِ گم شُده این رَه نَه به خود می‌پویَم

در پَسِ آیِنِه طوطی صِفَتَم داشته‌اند
آنچه اُستادِ اَزَل گُفت بگو می‌گویَم

مَن اگر خارَم و گَرگُل چَمَن آرایی هست
که از آن دَست که او می‌کِشَدَم می‌رویَم

دوستان عِیبِ منِ بی دِلِ حِیران مَکُنید
گوهَری دارَم و صاحِبِ نَظَری می‌جویَم

گَرچه با دَلقِ مُلَمَّعِ می گُلگون عِیب است
مَکُنَم عِیب کزو رَنگِ ریا می‌شویَم

خَندِه و گِریهٔ عُشّاق زِ جایی دِگَر است
می‌سُرایَم به شَب و وَقتِ سَحَر می‌مویَم

حافظَم گُفت که خاک درِ میخانه مَبوی
گو مَکُن عِیب که من مُشکِ خَتَن می‌بویَم

SIXTY-SEVEN

I've said it many times and I'll say it again:
I, the lost one, am not walking this road by myself.

I have been kept behind the mirror, and just like the parrot,
whatever the First Teacher tells me to say, I say.

Whether I am a thorn or rose depends on the gardener.
How he wants me to grow, I grow.

Friends, don't blame me for being overwhelmed and lost-hearted.
I have a jewel and seek an expert in gems.

It's wrong to drink red wine if you wear a mottled coat,
but don't blame me. With it I wash away the stain of hypocrisy.

The laughter and tears of lovers originate somewhere else.
I sing at night and at dawn I weep.

Háfiz said, "Don't bend down to sniff the dust of the tavern doorway."
Tell him, "Don't blame me. I smell the musk of Khotan."

شصت و هشت

گرچه ما بندگانِ پادشَهیم
پادشاهانِ مُلکِ صُبحگَهیم

گنج در آستین و کیسه تُهی
جامِ گیتی نَما و خاکِ رَهیم

هوشیارِ حُضور و مَستِ غُرور
بَحرِ توحید و غرقهٔ گُنَهیم

شاهدِ بَخت چون کِرشمه کُنَد
ماش آیینهٔ رُخ چو مَهیم

شاهِ بیدار بَخت را هَر شب
ما نِگهبانِ اَفسَر و کُلَهیم

گو غَنیمَت شُمار صُحبَتِ ما
که تو دَر خواب و ما به دیدهگَهیم

شاه مَنصور واقف است که ما
رویِ همَّت به هَر کُجا که نَهیم

دُشمنان را ز خون کَفَن سازیم
دوستان را قَبایِ فَتح دَهیم

رَنگِ تَزویر پیشِ ما نَبُوَد
شیرِ سُرخیم و اَفعیِ سیَهیم

وام حافظ بِگو که بازدِهَند
کِردَهایِ اِعتِراف و ما گوَهیم

SIXTY-EIGHT

Although we are slaves of the king
we rule the kingdom of dawn.

We have treasure in our sleeves but our purse is empty.
We are the world-revealing cup and the dust of the road.

We are sober in his presence and drunk with pride.
We are the sea of oneness and drowned in sin.

When good fortune, our beloved, winks at us
we are the mirror that reflects his moon face.

Every night we are the guardians of the crown and throne
of the king blessed by fortune.

Take advantage of our spiritual efforts
for while you sleep we stand watch.

Sháh Mansúr knows that
wherever we direct our spiritual efforts

we will wrap the enemy in shrouds of their own blood
and give the robe of victory to friends.

We do not carry with us the colors of hypocrisy.
We are the red lion and the black viper.

Tell them to pay Háfiz what is owed to him.
You promised, and I am a witness.

شصت و نه

خُدا را کَم نِشین با خِرقِه پوشان
رُخ از رِندانِ بی‌سامان مَپوشان

دَرین خِرقِه بَسی آلودِگی هست
خوشا وَقتِ قَبایِ می فُروشان

تو نازُک طَبعی و طاقَت نَیاری
گِرانی‌هایِ مُشتی دَلق پوشان

بیا وَز غَبنِ این سالوسیان بین
صُراحی خونِ دِل و بَربَط خُروشان

چو مَستم کَردِه‌ای مَستور مَنشین
چو نوشَم داده‌ای زَهرَم مَنوشان

درین صوفی وَشان دَردی نَدیدَم
که صافی بادِ عِیشِ دُرد نوشان

ز دِل گَرمیِّ حافظ بَر حَذر باش
که دارَد سینه‌ای چون دیگِ جوشان

SIXTY-NINE

For God's sake don't sit with the Sufis,
but don't hide your face from the indigent rends.

There is so much impurity in this Sufi cloak.
Hail to the pure cloak of the wine-sellers!

Your subtle nature can't endure
a handful of overbearing Sufis,

and look, because of these hypocrites' deceit
the flask's heart is filled with blood and the lute is crying.

Now that you've made me drunk, don't hide yourself from me.
Now that you have given me honey, don't make me drink poison.

In these pseudo-Sufis I saw no spiritual anguish.
May the joy of the dreg-drinkers be pure.

Beware the wrath of Háfiz's heart,
for it seethes in the boiling cauldron of his chest.

هفتاد

مَنَم که شُهرهٔ شَهرَم بِه عِشق وَرزیدَن
مَنَم که دیده نَیالوده‌ام بِه بَد دیدَن

به مِی پَرَستی ازآن نَقشِ خود بَرآب زَدَم
که تا خَراب کُنَم نَقشِ خود پَرَستیدَن

وَفا کُنیم و مَلامَت کِشیم و خوش باشیم
که در طَریقَتِ ما کافِریست رَنجیدَن

به پیرِ میکده گُفتَم که چیست راهِ نجات
بِخواست جامِ می و گُفت راز پوشیدَن

ز خَطِّ یار بیاموز مِهر با رُخِ خوب
که گِردِ عارِضِ خوبان خوش است گَردیدَن

مُرادِ دِل ز تَماشای باغِ عالَم چیست
به دَستِ مَردُمِ چَشم از رُخِ تو گُل چیدَن

عِنان به میکده خواهیم تافت زین مَجلِس
که وَعظِ بی‌عَمَلان واجِب است نَشنیدَن

به رَحمَتِ سَرِ زُلفِ تو واثِقَم وَرنه
کِشِش چو نَبوَد از آن سو چه سود کوشیدَن

مَبوس جُز لَبِ ساقی و جامِ می حافِظ
که دَستِ زُهد فُروشان خَطاسَت بوسیدَن

SEVENTY

In this town I am the one famous for being a lover.
I am the one who won't pollute his gaze by seeing evil.

I destroyed myself with wine-worship
to destroy any perception of self-worship.

I am loyal, endure scorn, and am happy,
for, on our path, to be offended is blasphemy.

I asked the elder of the tavern, "What is the path to salvation?"
He asked for a cup of wine and said, "To keep the secret."

Learn love from the trace of new down on the beauty's face
for to adore beautiful faces is a joy.

What does the heart want when it looks at the garden of the world?
To feast its eyes on the rose of your face.

From this preacher's flock I will head back to the tavern.
Thou shalt not listen to those who don't practice what they preach.

I believe in the compassion of your hair's curls.
Without their pull, what use is struggling?

Háfiz, don't kiss anything except the wine cup and her lips,
for it's a sin to kiss the hand of those who peddle piety.

هفتاد و یک

صُبح است ساقیا قَدَحی پُرشَراب کُن
دَورِ فَلَک دِرَنگ نَدارَد شِتاب کُن

زان پیشتَر که عالَم فانی شَوَد خَراب
ما را زِ جامِ بادهٔ گُلگُون خَراب کُن

خورشیدِ می ز مَشرِقِ ساغَر طُلوع کَرد
گر بَرگِ عَیش می‌طَلَبی تَرکِ خواب کُن

روزی که چَرخ از گِلِ ما کوزِه‌ها کُنَد
زِنهار کاسهٔ سَرِ ما پُرشَراب کُن

ما مَردِ زُهد و تَوبِه وُ طامات نیستیم
با ما به جامِ بادهٔ صافی خَطاب کُن

کارِ صَواب باده پَرَستیست حافِظا
بَرخیز و عَزمِ جَزم به کارِ صَواب کُن

SEVENTY-ONE

It's daybreak. O saqi, fill a cup with wine.
The wheel of heaven does not pause. Make haste.

Before this transient world is ruined
ruin me with a cup of ruby wine.

The sun of wine rose from the East of the cup.
If you seek what is needed for joy, give up sleep.

On the day that the universe makes a jug from my clay
don't hesitate: fill the cup of my skull with wine.

I am not a man of asceticism, exaggeration, and repentance.
If you address me, do so over a cup of pure wine.

O Háfiz, the right thing to do is worship wine. Get up,
and turn the face of resolve toward the right thing.

هفتاد و دو

چون شَوَم خاکِ رَهَش دامَن بیَفشانَد زِ مَن
وَر بِگویَم دل بگردان رو بگردانَد زِ مَن

روی رَنگین را به هَر کَس می‌نَماید هَمچو گُل
وَر بِگویَم بازپوشان بازپوشانَد زِ مَن

چَشمِ خود را گُفتَم آخر یِک نظر سیرَش ببین
گفت می‌خواهی مَگَر تا جوی خون رانَد زِ مَن

او به خونَم تِشنه وُ مَن بر لَبَش تا چون شَوَد
کام بِستانَم ازو یا داد بِستانَد زِ مَن

گَر چو شَمعَش پیش میرَم بَرغَمَم خندان شَوَد
وَر بِرَنجَم خاطرِ نازُک برنَجانَد زِ مَن

گَر چو فَرهادَم به تَلخی جان برآیَد باک نیست
بَس حکایَت‌های شیرین باز می‌مانَد زِ مَن

دوستان جان داده‌ام بَهرِ دَهانَش بنگرید
کو به چیزی مُختَصَر چون باز می‌مانَد زِ مَن

خَتم کُن حافظ که گَر زین دَست باشَد دَرسِ عشق
عقل دَر هَر گوشه‌ای افسانه‌یی خوانَد زِ مَن

SEVENTY-TWO

When I become dust on her path she shakes me from the hem of her skirt.
And if I say, "Have a change of heart!" she turns away.

Like the rose she shows her face to everyone.
And if I say, "Cover it!" she covers it from me.

I said to my own eye, "With a single glance, look your fill."
It said, "Not unless you want a river of blood to pour from me."

She thirsts for my blood and I thirst for her lip. Let's see:
will I take what I want from her or will she take her revenge on me?

If like a candle I die beside her, like morning she will laugh at my grief.
And if I am offended her delicate nature takes offense.

If I die in bitterness, like Farhad, I don't care,
because there will still be so many sweet stories about me.

Friends, I have given up my life for her mouth. See?
Such a trivial thing she denies me!

Enough, Háfiz. If this is the lesson of love
Reason will tell tall tales about me everywhere.

هفتاد و سه

وِصالِ او زِ عُمرِ جاودان بِه
خُداوَندا مَرا آن دِه کـه آن بِـه

بِه شَمشیرَم زَد و با کَس نَگُفتَم
که رازِ دوست از دُشمَن نَهان بِه

شَبی می‌گُفت چَشمِ کَس نَدیدَه‌ست
زِ مُرواریدِ گوشَم دَر جَهان بِه

خُدا را از طَبیبِ مَن بِپُرسید
که آخِر کِی شَوَد این ناتوان بِه

بِه خُلدَم دَعوَت ای زاهِد مَفَرما
که این سیبِ زَنَخ زان بوستان بِه

دِلا دایِم گِدایِ کویِ او باش
بِه حُکمِ آن که دَولَت جاودان بِه

بِه داغِ بَندِگی مُردَن بِدین دَر
بِه جانِ او که از مُلکِ جَهان بِه

جَوانا سَر مَتاب از پَندِ پیران
که رایِ پیر از بَختِ جوان بِه

اَگر چِه زِنده رود آبِ حیات است
وَلی شیرازِ ما از اِصفِهان بِه

گُلی کان پایمالِ سَروِ ما گَشت
بُوَد خاکش زِ خونِ اَرغَوان بِه

سُخَن اَندَر دَهانِ دوست شِکَّر
وَلیکَن گُفتهٔ حافِظ از آن بِه

SEVENTY-THREE

Union with him is better than eternal life.
O lord, give me that which is better.

He struck me with his sword and I told no one.
The friend's secret is better hidden from the enemy.

One night he said, "No one has seen in the world
anything better than the pearl of my ear."

For God's sake, ask my physician,
"When will this feeble one finally get better?"

O ascetic, don't summon me to heaven,
for the apple of his chin is better than that orchard.

O heart, be forever a beggar in his alleyway, for, as they say,
it's better to have wealth that is everlasting.

By his soul, it is better to die a slave on this threshold
than to rule the world.

O youth, don't shun the advice of your elders,
for the master's judgment is better than beginner's luck.

Although Zindehrúd is the water of life,
our Shiraz is better than Isfahan.

The dust of a rose trampled by our cypress
is prettier than the blood of the redbud tree.

In the mouth of the beloved speech is a jewel.
However, the verse of Háfiz is better than that.

هفتاد و چهار

دوش رَفتَم به دَرِ میکَدِه خواب آلوده
خِرقِه تَردامَن و سَجّادِه شَراب آلوده

آمَد اَفسوس کُنان مُغ بَچّهٔ بادِه فُروش
گفت بیدار شَو ای رَه رُو خواب آلوده

شُست و شویی کُن و آنگَه به خَرابات خَرام
تا نَگردَد زِ تو این دِیرِ خَراب آلوده

به هَوای لَبِ شیرین دَهَنان چَند کُنی
جَوهَرِ روح به یاقوتِ مُذاب آلوده

به طَهارَت گُذَران مَنزِلِ پیری و مَکُن
خِلعَتِ شیب چو تَشریفِ شَباب آلوده

آشنایانِ رَهِ عِشق دَرین بَحرِ عَمیق
غَرقِه گَشتَند و نَگَشتَند به آب آلوده

پاک و صافی شَو و از چاهِ طَبیعَت به دَرآی
که صَفایی نَدِهَد آبِ تُراب آلوده

گُفتَم ای جان و جَهان دَفتَرِ گُل عِیبی نیست
که شَوَد فَصلِ بَهار از مِی ناب آلوده

گُفت حافِظ لُغَز و نُکته به یارانِ مَفُروش
آه ازین لُطفِ به اَنواعِ عَتاب آلوده

SEVENTY-FOUR

Last night I went to the tavern door stained with sleep,
my coat-hem soaked, my prayer mat stained with wine.

The wine-seller's Magian boy came and shook his head
and said, "Wake up, sleepy traveler!

Wash yourself, and then stride into the tavern,
so you won't stain this cloister of ruin.

In your desire for sweet lips, for how long
will you stain the pearl of your spirit with melted ruby?

Remain pure in the waystation of old age,
and don't stain the mantle of age as you did the trappings of youth.

In this deep sea, those who knew love's road
were swamped but never touched by water.

Come forth clear and pure from the well of your nature,
for muddy water will not make you clean."

I said, "O my dear love, what can be wrong
if in springtime the book of the rose is stained with pure wine?"

He said, "Háfiz, don't peddle wisecracks and witticisms to the friends."
Ah, for this kindness, stained with so many kinds of reproach!

هفتاد و پنج

سَحَرگاهان که مَخمورِ شبانه
گِرِفتَم بادِه با چَنگ و چَغانه

نَهادَم عَقل را رَه توشِه از مِی
زِ شَهرِ هَستیَش کَردَم رَوانه

نِگارِ مِی فُروشَم عِشوه‌یی داد
که ایمِن گَشتَم از مَکرِ زَمانه

زِ ساقیِ کَمان اَبرو شِنیدَم
که ای تیرِ مَلامَت را نِشانه

نَبَندی زان میان طَرفی کَمروار
اَگَر خود را بِبینی در میانه

بُرو این دام بَر مُرغی دِگَر نِه
که عَنقا را بُلَند است آشیانه

نَدیم و مُطرِب و ساقی هَمه اوست
خیالِ آب و گِل دَر رَه بَهانه

بِدِه کَشتیِ مِی تا خوش بِرانیم
ازین دَریایِ ناپیدا کَرانه

وُجودِ ما مُعمّاییست حافظ
که تَحقیقَش فُسون است و فَسانه

SEVENTY-FIVE

At dawn, still half-drunk from the night before,
I drank wine to the sound of harp and chaghaneh.

I gave Reason wine as provisions for his journey
and sent him away from the city of existence.

The lovely wine-seller gave me an amorous glance
that made me feel safe from the deceit of the material world.

From the saqi with the bow-shaped brow I heard,
"O you who are the target of the arrow of reproach,

if you imagine you exist
you will gain nothing.

Go, and set this snare for a different bird,
for the *anqá*'s nest is out of reach.

The intimate friend, the minstrel, and the saqi are all him.
On this road, the illusion of an Adam is just an excuse."

Give me a vessel of wine so that we may sail happily across this sea
toward the shore we can't yet see.

Our existence is a riddle, Háfiz.
Trying to solve it is just fairytale and illusion.

هفتاد و شش

با مُدَّعی مَگویید اَسرارِ عِشق و مَستی
تا بی خَبَر بِمیرَد در دردِ خود پَرَستی

عاشِق شَو اَر نَه روزی کارِ جَهان سَرآیَد
ناخوانده نَقشِ مَقصود از کارگاهِ هَستی

دوش آن صَنَم چه خوش گُفت در مَجلسِ مُغانَم
با کافِرانَ چه کارَت گر بُت نمی‌پَرَستی

سُلطانِ من خُدا را زُلفَت شِکَست ما را
تا کی کُنَد سیاهی چَندین درازدَستی

در گوشهٔ سَلامَت مَستور چون تَوان بود
تا نَرگِسِ تو با ما گویَد رُموزِ مَستی

آن روز دیده بودَم این فِتنه‌ها که بَرخاست
کز سَرکِشیِ زَمانی با ما نمی‌نِشَستی

عِشقَت به دَستِ طوفان خواهَد سِپُرد حافِظ
چون بَرقِ ازین کَشاکِش پِنداشتی که جَستی

SEVENTY-SIX

Don't reveal to the adversary the secrets of love and drunkenness
so that he will die ignorant, in the pain of his own self-worship.

Fall in love, otherwise one day you will die
without having read what has been written about the goal of creation.

Last night in the Magi's assembly how nicely the idol put it:
"If you are not an idolater, why are you here among the unbelievers?"

By God, my king, the curls of your hair have broken us.
For how long will that blackness oppress?

How can one hide in the corner of righteousness
if your eyes speak the secret of drunkenness?

I foresaw all of these calamities the day that,
out of pride, you refused to sit next to me.

Love will throw you into the storm, Háfiz.
You thought that, like lightning, you had leaped out of this maelstrom.

هفتاد و هفت

دو یارِ زیرَک و از بادهٔ کُهَن دومَنی
فَراغتیّ و کِتابیّ و گوشهٔ چَمَنی

مَن این مَقام به دُنیا و آخِرَت نَدهَم
اَگَرچه دَر پیِ‌اَم اُفتَند هَردَم اَنجُمَنی

که هَرکه کُنجِ قِناعَت به گَنجِ دنیا داد
فُروخت یوسُفِ مِصری به کَمتَرین ثَمَنی

بیا که رَونَقِ این کارخانه کَم نَشَوَد
به زُهدِ هَمچو تویی یا به فِسقِ همچو مَنی

زِ تُندبادِ حَوادِث نِمی‌تَوان دیدَن
درین چَمَن که گُلی بودِه است یا سَمَنی

بِبین دَر آینهٔ جام نَقش بَندی غِیب
که کَس به یاد نَدارَد چُنین عَجَب زَمَنی

ازین سُموم که بَر طَرفِ بوستان بُگذَشت
عَجَب که بوی گُلی هَست و رَنگِ نَسترَنی

به صَبر کوش تو ای دِل که حَق رَها نَکُنَد
چُنین عَزیز نِگینی به دَستِ اَهرِمَنی

مِزاجِ دَهر تَبَه شُد درین بَلا حافظ
کُجاسَت فِکرِ حکیمی و رای بَرهَمَنی

SEVENTY-SEVEN

Two refined friends and two jugs of old wine,
a quiet moment with a book in the corner of a meadow—

I would not exchange these for this world or the next
even if a crowd tries to persuade me otherwise,

because whoever trades the corner of contentment for the treasure of the world
sold Joseph of Egypt for a song.

Know that all creation will never be diminished
by asceticism like yours or debauchery like mine.

Given the whirlwind of calamities, you cannot see
that this field once held roses and jasmine.

See, in the mirror of the cup that is a reflection of the invisible,
that no one remembers a time as strange as this.

And given the *simoom* that has swept through this garden,
how can there still be the scent of the rose and the color of jasmine?

Try to stay patient, O heart, for God would never leave
such a precious gem in the hands of an Ahriman.

This disaster destroyed the well-being of the world, Háfiz.
Where is the Greek physician's cure? Where is the Brahmin's ruling?

هفتاد و هشت

این خِرقِه که مَن دارَم در رَهنِ شَراب اولی
وین دَفتَرِ بی مَعنی غَرقِ مِی ناب اولی

چون عُمر تَبَه کَردَم چَندان که نِگَه کَردَم
در کنجِ خَراباتی اُفتادِه خَراب اولی

چون مَصلِحَت اَندیشی دور است زِ دَرویشی
هَم سینه پُر از آتَش هَم دیدِه پُرآب اولی

مَن حالتِ زاهِد را با خَلق نَخواهَم گُفت
این قِصِّه اگَر گویَم با چَنگ و رَباب اولی

تا بی سَر و پا باشَد اوضاعِ فَلَک زین دَست
در سَرِ هَوَسِ ساقی در دَستِ شَراب اولی

از هَمچو تو دِلداری دِل بَرنَکَنَم آری
چون تاب کِشَم باری زان زُلفِ به تاب اولی

چون پیر شُدی حافظ از میکده بیرون آی
رِندی و هَوَسناکی در عَهدِ شَباب اولی

SEVENTY-EIGHT

This cloak I have is better pawned for wine
and this meaningless book is better drowned in it.

Now that I look back at my wasted life
it is better to have fallen down drunk in the tavern corner.

Prudence and proper thoughts lie far from the dervish way.
Better to fill your breast with fire and your eye with tears.

I will tell no one about the ascetic's indiscretions.
To tell this story I need rebab and harp.

As long as the heavens remain so insolent
it's better to have your mind on the saqi and your hand on the wine.

No, I will never let go of a love like you.
Since I must burn, better that it be because of your curly hair.

You have grown old, Háfiz, so come out of the tavern.
Revelry and the rend's life are better suited to the days of youth.

هفتاد و نه

ای بی خَبَر بِکوش که صاحِب خَبَر شَوی
تا راهرو نباشی کِی راهبَر شوی

در مَکتَبِ حَقایق پیشِ ادیبِ عشق
هان ای پِسَر بِکوش که روزی پِدَر شَوی

دست از مِسِ وُجود چو مَردانِ رَه بشَوی
تا کیمیای عِشق بیابیّ و زَر شَوی

خواب و خورَت زِ مَرتَبهٔ خویش دور کَرد
آنگه رِسی به خویش که بی خواب و خور شَوی

گر نورِ عِشقِ حَق به دِل و جانَت اوفتَد
باالله کز آفتابِ فَلَک خویتَر شَوی

یک دَم غَریقِ بَحرِ خُدا شَو گُمان مَبَر
کز آبِ هَفت بَحر به یک موی تَر شَوی

از پای تا سَرَت هَمه نورِ خُدا شَوَد
در راهِ ذوالجَلال چو بی پا و سَر شَوی

وَجهِ خُدا اگر شَوَدَت مَنظَرِ نَظَر
زین پَس شَکی نَماند که صاحِب نَظَر شَوی

بُنیادِ هَستیِ تو چو زیر و زِبَر شَوَد
در دِل مَدار هیچ که زیر و زِبَر شَوی

گر دَر سَرَت هَوای وِصال است حافظا
باید که خاکِ دَرگَهِ اَهلِ نَظَر شَوی

SEVENTY-NINE

O ignorant one, try to become a master of knowledge.
If you are not a traveler, how can you become a guide?

In the school of truth listen carefully to the tutor of love
so that one day, O son, you can become a father.

Like those worthy of the path, wash your hands of the copper of existence
so that you can find the philosopher's stone of love and become gold.

Sleeping and eating have kept you far from your station.
You will find yourself when you give up sleeping and eating.

If the light of the love for truth shines on your heart and soul,
by God, you will become lovelier than the sun in heaven.

For a moment drown yourself in the sea of God and don't believe
that the seven seas will wet a single hair.

From head to toe you will become the light of God
when you lose yourself on His glorious road.

Once God's face becomes the object of your sight
there is no doubt that you will become a master of vision.

When the foundations of your existence become topsy-turvy
don't worry at all about being topsy-turvy.

O Háfiz, if desire for union fills your head
you must become dust in the doorway of those who see.

هشتاد

در هَمـه دِیرِ مُغان نیست چو مَن شیدایی
خِرقِه جایی گِروِ باده وُ دَفتَر جایی

دل کـه آیینـهٔ شـاهیست غُباری دارَد
از خُدا می‌طَلَبَم صُحبَتِ روشَـن رایی

کردِه‌ام تَوبِه بِه دَستِ صَنَم بادِه فُروش
که دِگر می نَخورَم بی‌رُخِ بَزم آرایی

جویها بَستـه‌ام از دیده بِه دامان که مَگَر
در کِنـارَم بِنِشـانَند سَـهـی بالایی

کَشتـیِ بادِه بیاوَر که مَرا بی رُخِ دوست
گَشت هَر گوشهٔ چَشـم از غَمِ دِل دَریایی

شَـرحِ این قِصّـه مَگَر شَمـع بَرآرَد بِه زَبان
وَرنَه پَروانـه نَدارَد بِه سُـخَن پَروایی

نَـرگِس اَر لاف زد از شیوهٔ چَشـمِ تو مَرَنج
نَرَوَند اَهلِ نَظَـر از پـی نابینـایی

سُخَنِ غِیر مَگو بـا مَنِ مَعشوقه پَرَست
کز وی و جامِ می‌اَم نیست بِه کَس پَروایی

این حَدیثَم چِه خوش آمَد که سَحَرگَه می‌گفت
بر دَرِ میکدِه‌ای بـا دَف و نـی تَرسـایی

گَر مُسَلمانی ازیـن است که حافظ دارد
آه اَگَـر از پـی امـروز بُـوَد فَردایی

EIGHTY

In the entire monastery of the Magi no one is as love-sick as I.
My cloak is pawned for wine in one place and my book in another.

My heart, a mirror for kings, is covered with dust.
I ask God for the company of a clear-sighted companion.

To the wine-selling idol I have made a vow of repentance:
I won't drink wine unless with a lovely reveler.

I have let streams flow from my eyes to the hem of my skirt hoping
that a tall slender cypress will sit down beside me.

Bring a vessel of wine, for without the friend's face
my eyes have become an ocean of sorrow.

Perhaps the candle will reveal the secret of this story,
because the moth has no desire to speak.

If the narcissus boasts that she has your amorous glance, don't be offended.
People of insight won't follow in the footsteps of the blind.

I worship the beloved. Don't speak to me of anyone else.
I care only for her and a cup of wine.

How much I liked this happy story a Christian sang at dawn
accompanied by drum and flute at the tavern door:

"If Háfiz is an example of a good Muslim,
woe if after today there is a tomorrow!"

AFTERWORD:
THE VISIONARY TOPOGRAPHY OF HÁFIZ[1]

DARYUSH SHAYEGAN

Khwája Shams ud-Dín Muhammad Háfiz-i Shírází, the Persian poet of the fourteenth century, is one of the greatest mystics and lyrical poets of all time. The Iranian tradition has designated him the *lisán-al-ghayb*, "the tongue of the Invisible" and *tarjumán al-asrár*, "the interpreter of the mysteries." And this for good reason, for of all the poets who have written in Persian—and there are very many of them—he has enjoyed the most privileged position, being, as it were, the intimate interlocutor of every heart in distress, of every soul that is seized by mystical exaltation. It is no accident therefore that Persians often consult his *Díwán*, in the same way that the Chinese consult the *I Ching*.

Being the interpreter of the mysteries, Háfiz is also an undisputed master of spiritual hermeneutic (*ta'wíl*); I would even say that his vision is fashioned of the *ta'wíl*, as the poet not only searches into the unfathomable mysteries which open up thanks to the divine theophanies, but he is himself the locus where these same theophanies unveil themselves. This vision is reflected as much in the structure of his ghazals as in the almost magical perfection of his word, and in the sovereign art with which he maintains complete and undisputed mastery over all the resources and nuances of the Persian language. This vision is such that the art of the mystical lyric reaches an apotheosis that has never been surpassed: he marks both the supreme flowering and the uttermost limit of his art.

---

[1] The visionary Topography of Háfiz" was delivered at the 1980 session of l'Université Saint Jean de Jérusalem and published in Cahier No. 7, *L'Hermeneutique Permanente* (Paris: Berg International), adapted from the French by Lana and Peter Russell for the journal, *Temenos*.

All the millenary genius of Persian art: the judicious equilibrium between form and content, the economy of means, the striking concision of paradoxical ideas, the affective and polyvalent tonalities of verbal magic amplifying itself on several registers, the polymorphic correspondences of many alluring images in the world's mirrors, condense miraculously in his art. This is why Háfiz is not simply a great Persian poet, he is the "miracle" of Persian literature; it is in him that the millenary sap of the culture is crystallized, which grafting the prophetic tradition of the Muhammadan Revelation on to the ancient spirit of Iran, made a synthesis so full, so profound, that it became, as it were, the *humanitias* of all Islam, oriental and Iranian.

Every Persian has a private bond with Háfiz. It matters little whether he is learned, mystic, unlettered, or *rend* (inspired libertine), as Háfiz called himself. Every Persian finds in him a part of himself, discovers in him an unexplored niche in his own memory, a fragrant recollection from the interior garden of which he is the unique guardian. It is from this communion that the poet's tomb is a place of pilgrimage for all Persians. Everyone goes there to seek be it but a particle of his presence: humble people from the bazaar, minor officials, intellectuals, poets, ragged beggars, all go there to collect themselves and to receive the poet's message in the silence of their heart.

How is it that Iran's most esoteric poet should also be the most popular? How do we reconcile this symbolic language with a popularity which makes the poet intimate Friend in every household? This popularity does not owe so much to the clarity of his language as to the occult correspondence which it awakens in every heart that hearkens to his call: every listener seems to find in it an answer to his question, every reader thinks he is discovering an allusion to his desire, every man finds in him a sympathetic interlocutor capable of understanding his secret, and of harmonizing it with the modulations of his song. For example, love assumes different forms according to whether it is envisaged on one level or another. It will be passionate and earthly love for some, and a profound nostalgia in quest of their original soil for others; and it will be the divine Beloved for all those who, opening themselves to what lies behind the veil of symbols, attain to a level of first events. Hence this "connivance" of the poet with all his readers, whatever register and level they belong to.

Thus, the understanding of his hearers varies according to their knowledge, their sensibility, but each receives his or her due and no one goes away empty. With the reading of Háfiz, as with the Qur'án, the less one comprehends intellectually, the more one receives spiritually. By the associations of shaded tonalities endlessly reverberating on the keyboards of the senses, transmuting correspondences into synchronic states amplified more and more, this poetry penetrates the heart, creating a juxtaposition of states of the soul, by which the receptive soul and symbolic tenor of the poem harmonize in the coincidence of the moment, so that this synchronicity of symbol and soul becomes the mystical configuration of a precise state.

This is also due to the particular structure of the ghazal itself. The reader has the impression that the poet has an eye "with multiple facets"; the world no longer unfolds itself in a simultaneous blossoming. Each distich is a complete whole, a world; within the ghazal one distich is not joined chronologically to the next, but is synchronically consubstantial with it. It is like a world within a larger world, which forms an integral part of the *Díwán*, as this latter forms an integral part of the cosmic vision of the poet. So, from one distich to the next, the same tonalities are amplified on extended registers, calling forth magical correspondences at every level.

The source of the energy of the poetic vision is the eye of the poet's heart, which is at once both the point of origin of all the soul's vibrations, and the center which "spatializes" the vision. This synchronic coincidence of planes of vision is the beginning of the soul's dialectic movement, since the limitations of the vision are made good by a continual flow back and forth between the heart of the poet and the primeval source from which he draws his inspiration. In other words, a perpetual oscillation between self-revelation of the Divine in its self-concealment, and the concealment of the Divine in its self-revelation; between a Beauty that attracts as it repels and a Majesty that repels as it attracts. Why is the heart the starting point of this movement? Because, as Háfiz says as he addresses the Beloved:

> Thou hast set the Treasure of Love in our ravaged heart,
> Thou hast thrown the shadow of fortune over the ruined corner.

Here we encounter three essential symbols of the dialectic of love in the work of Háfiz: that is to say, the dispenser of the Treasure of Love, Love itself, and the ravaged heart. This Treasure, the poet adds, is also a profound sorrow (*gham*), a poignant nostalgia:

> The Lord of pre-eternity (*sultán-í-azal*) offers us the Treasure of
> Sorrow (*ganj-i gham-i 'ishq*)
> That we may descend into this ravaged dwelling (*manzil-i wiráneh*).

Let us look at the connotations of the symbolism of the heart in speculative gnosis. The heart, says the Islamic mystic, is the Throne of Mercy, and Shaykh Muhammad Láhíjí, who wrote the famous commentary on Mahmud Shabestarí's *Rose Garden of Mystery* (*Gulshan-i Ráz*), adds, "just as in the outside world, the Throne is the epiphany of the name of Mercy, likewise in the interior world it is the heart (*qalb*) that is its epiphany. At every breath of the Merciful One, God manifests himself in a new theophany in the heart of the believer."

The heart of a human being is always in motion (the word *qalb* in Arabic means both "heart" and "revolution" in the sense of inversion); a motion that manifests itself in terms of renewal and resurrection at every instant, and which works in such a way that the instant of disappearance coincides immediately with the appearance of its counterpart. The heart is therefore the center of the Throne and the Throne in its periphery; being the initial point of epiphany, it is also the center which calls into being the space of vision. It is for this reason, says Háfiz, that the heart holds the cup of Jam, the cup of cosmic vision, which is also the mirror reflecting the invisible world (*ghayb namá*). But the heart is also ravaged with wounds (*majrúh*) as it broods longingly over the stigmata inflicted on it by the Beloved, and acts as a shield against the innumerable arrows that the Beloved's brows let loose. The heart is also purple with the flame of Love and bears as a mark of devotion the "scar of the tulip" (*dagh-i lála*). This scar, says Háfiz "which we have placed in our heart is able to set ablaze the harvest of a hundred rational devout worshippers."

These three essential symbols: The Lord of pre-eternity, the sorrow of love, and the ravaged heart, raise us immediately to the level of the first theophanies, and bring us within the orbit of the famous divine saying according to which God said:

> I was a hidden treasure, I longed to be known.
> So I created the creation, in order that I should be known.

God is a Hidden Treasure, that is, an unfathomable essence in the Mystery of Ipseity. But this treasure longs to be known, and initially in His innermost heart a strong desire manifests itself, a nostalgia to reveal Himself; then comes the second stage which fulfills this desire and designates the Names that were concealed in the undifferentiated Thought of God.

Every Name of God aspires to be made manifest, this is what the concept of God's nostalgia and His Love of manifesting himself (*hub-i hudúrí*) conveys; it demands an epiphany, a mirror in which it can be reflected: the knower (*'álim*) aspires to be known (*ma'lúm*). This mutual aspiration, this sympathy between Archetypes striving to be invested with the Divine Presence and Names seeking a mirror to contemplate themselves in, constitutes the second visionary theophany (*shuhúdí*), or the marriage of Names and Attributes. But the Archetypes are mirrors of Divine Beauty and the image reflected in them is the world. To this two way movement—the longing of the hidden Treasure to reveal itself in creatures, and the Love of these creatures, aspiring to be united to the Names of which they are epiphanies—correspond the two arcs of descent (*qaws-i nuzúlí*) and ascent (*qaws-i 'urújí*). The descent symbolizes ceaseless influx of Being; the ascent symbolizing the return movement to God; the former symbolizes the creation in a recurrent and never-failing effusion, the latter the resurrections of beings and their return to their initial and final cause. The cosmic vision of the poet opens into the space between these two arcs, the one originating from the pre-eternity of God (*azal*), and the other starting out from man himself to flow into post-eternity (*abad*).

I. BETWEEN PRE-ETERNITY AND POST-ETERNITY

It is in alluding to this same space between *azal* and *abad* that the poet says:

> From the Dawn of the first Beginning till the twilight of the last End,
> Friendship and Love have drawn inspiration from one sole pact,
> one single trust.

Here we enter upon Háfiz's visionary topography, arriving at a world whose co-ordinates are not ordered in the quantitative time of chronological events, and which consequently is neither historical, nor linear, nor progressive, but a world in the interior of which every event is presence, and every duration is an instant of this presence. Unquestionably, with regard to the eternity of the Divine itself, the pre-eternal and post-eternal have no meaning, since in its Essence, pre- and post- coincide in the indeterminacy of the divine Ipseity. They take on meaning only in relation to the shadow of God, in relation to that Other-than-God which, while it is a veil obscuring His face, remains no less a necessary expedient of His self-revelation. God and humanity are the poles of creation; it is between these two poles—one the Origin with regard to descent and the other the Origin with regard to return—that pre- and post-eternity derive all their direction and meaning.

Without the creation of human beings, who took upon themselves the destiny of his folly, there would have been neither initial nor final point, there would have been only the occult eternity of the Hidden Treasure. To see the world as a respite between the initial point and the final point of the cycle of Being is already to anticipate one's return, indeed one's eschatology; it is also to participate in that "play of the magical glance" (*kirishma-i jádú*), in that the cycle of love thanks to which the two-way movement of the two arcs developing in opposite directions, sets the cosmic wheel of Being turning.

In this state, the poet is established at the center of Being and, as it were, sets the wheel of Love turning. And even while it remains immobile in bewilderment (*sargashta-i pábarjá*) his heart nonetheless spins about in all directions like the needle of a compass. Having become in this way a visionary witness to this play of love, he is the outlet where "the twin tresses of the Eternal Beloved" (*sar-zulfayn-i yár*) are united. It follows that this witnessing is a cosmic vision (*díd-i jahánbín*) which contemplates the play of the cycle of Love turning without respite in the instantaneous succession of a presence that is also, for Háfiz, a co-presence in this Play; and co-attendance at the cosmogonic events of the genesis of the world; that is to say, an act of foundation. For in being present at the first cosmogonic events, the poet is not merely present at these events but, participating in this act, he lays the foundations, through his word, of the world, and assumes a demiurgic role. "Come," he says, "let us split apart the domed ceiling of the celestial spheres, and let us lay the foundation of a new structure." It is by virtue of the nature of this co-presence at, and co-foundation of, the first events that the poet peoples with symbols the visionary space that blossoms, like a primordial lotus, between *azal* and *abad*.

Háfiz is unquestionably the most original of all philosophical poets. He never turns his gaze from the primeval focus whence all inspiration comes to him. Every glance for him is a glance only insofar as it opens like a magic lamp in the Niche of Prophetic Lights. Every drunkenness is drunkenness only insofar as it drinks deep of the wine of the primordial tavern. Every head of hair is a head of hair only insofar as the waving chain of its tresses binds up again and commemorates the alliance of the primordial Pact (*'ahd-i alast*). Every morning breeze is a breeze only insofar as it brings to us a fragrant breath from the Quarter of the Friend (*kúy-i dúst*). All his attention, joy, and senses are tense for the space of that unique moment that is granted where every light is a divine theophany, every cup of wine a reflection of the Face of the Beloved, as well as the form of the azure bowl of the sky. Every resemblance is a re-actualization of the primordial memory. His whole soul is present in this sacred space where being is mythogenesis and the event an archetypal act in the dawn of the eternal beginning. And it is as a Seer casting his gaze over the "garden of the world" (*bágh-i jahán*) that he would gather, "thanks to the hand of the pupil of his eye, a flower from the Face of Beloved."

The eye of the poet, illuminated by the eye of the Beloved, sees in this garden the world unveiling itself as the dazzling face of the Beloved, and also becoming clouded over like its dusky hair that darkens its resplendence and makes it appear like "darkened day" (*rúz-i tárík*). This oscillation, between Beauty's occultation and self-revelation and its self-revelation and occultation, is conveyed in a number of Háfiz's ghazals by the "Night of Separation" (*shab-i hijrán*) and the "Day of the Union" (*rúz-i wasl*); for every separation is great with an imminent union, and every union potentially conceals a separation. This succession of repulsion and attraction, which mutually provoke each other, engenders the dialectic movement of Love, and the ascent of nostalgia that permeates all Persian mystical poetry. Here are some examples from Háfiz:

> How am I to spread my wing in the span of thy Union,
> For its feathers are shed already in the nest of separation.

And in another place:

In this dark night I have lost the path of the quest.
Come, then, O star that guides us.
Go where I may, my anguish does but grow—
Beware this desert, this endless road.

II. THE AESTHETIC COORDINATES OF THE VISIONARY WORLD

Let us see now how Háfiz goes about furnishing this space which opens up between *azal* and *abad*; what, in other words, are the aesthetic consequences of this visionary topography. It goes without saying that we shall scarcely be able to analyze the whole bewitching aesthetic of his poetic world; but we may try to reveal some themes, some modalities of his expression.

Let us say at the outset that the visionary space between *azal* and *abad* comprehends the entire topography of Being itself; that is to say, the ontological hierarchy of the superimposed worlds: the *jabarút* as well as the *malakút*, the world of Archetypal Images, of which Henry Corbin has spoken, as well as the world of sensible phenomena. But for Háfiz, who is a mystic and above all a poet, the question is posed not in terms of conceptual explication but in the form of poetic license, and by the elaboration of a whole magic of symbolic forms suited to convey the polyvalence of what, to the last, remains ineffable, beyond any form of expression. In Háfiz, all things come together to translate the untranslatable, to express the inexpressible, and to do this he has recourse not only to the structure of the ghazal itself—which unfolds itself like concentric circles progressively amplifying at each reprise the resonance of spiritual states, and which, because of its drastic limits, demands a polishing of thought to the point of transparency—but Háfiz exploits to the full all the virtuosities and subtleties of the Persian language, such as pairs of opposites, correlative terms, word play, homonyms, etymological contrivances, rhythmical alliterations, cadenced assonances, so enhancing the webs of symbols which each reflect.

1) There is in the first place a whole constellation of visual images connected with divine Beauty; symbolized by the most alluring features of the Eternal Feminine, such as the flowing locks which by a backward movement, like the arc of ascent, bind the lover once more to the initial place where the first knot, the first lock of that hair, is tied; and this

lock is an Alliance (*paymán*) that the poet vows never to betray or turn aside from. The eyebrow of the Beloved symbolizes sometimes the arched prayer-niche (*mihráb-i-abrú*); sometimes the bow which lets loose the arrows of her lashes; sometimes the arched roof of the temple of vision of pre-eternity; that is to say, before the ceiling of the vault of heaven had yet been set in place. The beauty-spot is in keeping with the unitary vision of the world. This "black point" is, the poet says, "but the image of thy beauty-spot in the garden of vision."

Starting from the aesthetic elements of the Eternal Feminine, the visionary topography of the poet is in broad outline formed: the topography of the land of the Friend (*kishwar-i dúst*), which has its lanes, quarters, prayer niche, its *ka'ba*, *qibla*, hours of contemplation, and garden of ecstasy; whence rises that fine dust which serves as collyrium for his eyes; whence flow the images that throng his imagination; whence rise aloft the messages that come to him, sometimes on the breezes of *sabá* (morning) caressing him at the hour of dawn when the candle burns low, sometimes in the cup-bearer's vermilion cup, sometimes in the song of the hoopoe. In Háfiz these varied images express the symbol of the divine messenger that we meet again in the form of a youth or angel in the visionary narratives of Avicenna and Suhrawardi; in the form of the Holy Spirit, assimilated to the Active Intelligence in the philosophers; and it is once again the idea of this messenger which is symbolized by the office of mediator that falls to the Angel Gabriel in prophetic revelation. This topography also delineates a whole region of the heart that the poet names *hawá-yi dil* (literally, the weather of the heart), and which constitutes the human configuration of the spiritual realm of *malakút* to which the poet aspires, and in relation to which the world is only an illusion, a snare. Háfiz says:

> Her hair is a trap, her beauty-spot the bait in the trap,
> And I in quest of the bait, have fallen into the trap.

2) In its auditory and narrative form, this visionary space is also a story of Love (*qissa-yi 'ishq*) or the story of a passionate sorrow (*qissa-yi ghussa*); an eternal dialogue between lover and Beloved, one and the same story which is never repeated in exactly the same way, and each narration of which is taken up in a new and hitherto unexpressed form since it recounts the story of a unique soul in search of its Beloved. Háfiz says:

> The nostalgia of Love is always one and the same story,
> But at every hearing is made new.

But this story goes back to the "story" of an original recital, to a first revelation:

> Behind the mirror I have been made to be like the parrot:
> I repeat what the Lord of pre-eternity has ordered me to say.

Just as every vision is illuminated at the Niche of Prophetic Lights, as every hearing is a hearkening to the original Utterance, as every story of love is a differentiated, particularized version of this same original Utterance, so each presence at the first event is also the remembrance of an alliance whose prolonged echoes constitute the chain of memory, and which the illusory attraction of the world often makes us forget. All of the senses: touch, sight, taste, and, in particular, smell (because of the recollective powers of this latter are singularly evocative), are combined in extremely subtle, finely shaded proportions in order to awaken, each in its own way, the memory of the Friend, like the sound of bells of the caravan in the desert, the aromatic musk of the Tartary gazelle, the exquisite aroma of wine, the sweet balm strewn by the messenger wind, so that the fragrant sap of his memory pervades the whole soul of the poem and creates that almost magical space in which images, whatever sensible object they belong to, coincide synchronically to weave the web of this immemorial memory.

3) If the world is impregnated with the memory of the Friend, this memory is also the recollection of a drunkenness, of a cup drunk in pre-eternity within the primordial Tavern:

> Last night I saw the angels knocking at the tavern door,
> Modeling the clay of man, becoming drunk with the original wine;
> The inhabitants of the sacred enclosure and of the divine *malakút*
> Drank from one cup with me, the pilgrim.

If then the angels have mixed the clay of humanity with the wine of mercy, humans carry within themselves the quintessence of that first drunkenness and, drinking from the cup in the tavern of the Magi, do but receive from the cup-bearer what was destined for them from the beginning. But to receive that which was from all time due to us is tantamount to assuming our destiny; it is also tantamount to commemorating the act by virtue of which it was destined for us. It follows from this that the entire universe becomes a tavern fragrant with all the wine of merciful Being; and all creatures, all the "drunken ones" of the tavern of the Magi, are like so many cups, and each of them receives, according to the capacity which is his lot, a drop of that delicious drink; and the drunkenness from that drink lasts until the resurrection. As Háfiz says:

> Whoever has drunk like me a draught from the cup of the Friend
> Shall not become sober until the dawn of resurrection.

The images relating to the tavern, to cups, to the cup-bearer, are so many symbols which, grafted on to the aesthetic ground of the Eternal Feminine, give rise to this erotico-mystic and Bacchic symbolism of the poet of Shiraz, which is so alluring, and which (alas!) often leads to shallow and hedonist interpretations of his poetry. That there is no antagonism between earthly wine and divine wine, just as there is none between profane love and the love of God, since one is the necessary initiation to the other, is what Háfiz intends to show. He not only exalts sensible beauty and "earthly nourishment," he transmutes them, thanks to the incantation of his word, into a divine and fantastic banquet at which angels become cup-bearers drunk with love, like those ravishing and lascivious nymphs we admire in the form of *apsáras* in the Buddhist grottoes at Ajanta and Ellora.

4) All these different modalities of sensible expression: sight, hearing, taste, as well as smell, converge, finally in the memory of an event which is a sort of alliance which itself constitutes man, as well as his destiny. What then is the meaning of this Alliance to which we have referred? Háfiz says:

> The heavens could not bear the burden of this Charge (*bár-i amánat*)
> And the winning lot, the Trust, falls to me, the fool.

This Lot is the burden of the Charge (*amánat*) entrusted to man at the beginning; man is, in other words, the repository of the universality of the Names and Attributes, in accordance with this Quranic verse, which says:

> We offered [the Trust] to the heavens, to the earth and to the

mountains. They refused to take it upon themselves and they were afraid of it; and man assumed it for he is dark (*zalúman*) and ignorant (*jahúlan*). (Qur'an 33:72)

And in the exegesis of the mystics this means: we offered that repository of the universal to Heaven, symbolizing the Spirits, to Earth, representing material bodies, and to the Mountains, symbolizing the world of Archetypal Images; we appealed to their ontological fitness, but they set themselves against it, being unfit to do it, while man had the capacity; that is to say, according to Háfiz, he was foolish enough to take on a responsibility that the entire universe refused.

Háfiz's openness to the space of memory, as well as his witnessing of events which are so mingled with the mythical dawn of every beginning, work in such a way that the poet, while still in this world, is beleaguered by another world, and while still captive in the snare of illusions, he remains nonetheless the free bird of the garden of visions. This perpetual shuttle between two orders of existence, the one partaking of the free flight of the bird initiated into the "rose-garden of the sacred," and the other mingled with the lamentations of captivity, betrays a paradoxical position which remains inherent in the ambivalent situation of the Seer himself. The poet knows that he belongs to the world of *malakút*, that there is his dwelling-place, the more so as all the epiphanies he contemplates unceasingly invite him there; but he also knows that he has fallen into the cage of earthly existence. Now and then the poet acknowledges his powerlessness to take his flight towards the vertiginous heights.

> How shall I turn within the space of the world of Sanctity
> Since in the alcove of combination [of elements] I remain nailed to my body.

The effect of the oscillating position of Háfiz between the world of sanctity and the fall into "time" is that his position expresses on the plane of the spatial movement of the poetic vision that which at the ethical level of *gnosis* remains the paradoxical status of the liberated sage. The poet remains suspended between two manners of apprehending things: having one foot in the other world and one foot in this world; it is with the eschatological bias of the former that he will see this world unfolding itself before his eyes. That is, the time of the poet's presence lies between *abad* and *azal* and is therefore an unveiling; but to this visionary time-space Háfiz opposes a horizontal, linear time which runs between the two shores of the world.

> From shore to shore the host of darkness stretches,
> From *azal* to *abad* opens the dervishes' respite.

His paradoxical situation comes precisely from the crossing of these two times, one of which flows out into post-eternity (*abad*) completing the cycle of Being, while the other establishes the horizon of becoming on the linear plane. It is with regard to this horizontal time that the world is a lure, an illusion, a snare; and to emphasize all this futile trumpery, Háfiz uses the image of the new bride.

> The world in its outward form is like a new bride,
> But whoever cleaves to it offers his life as dowry.

Or again, the world is a ravishing bride, but be warned that this "chaste and modest one becomes the bride of none," and her infidelity knows no limit. These negative aspects of the world, likened to infidelity, inconstancy, and the fleeting attractions of a beauty which is evanescent, are connected with guile and deceit because this world, despite being bride (*'arús*), is nonetheless an old woman (*'ajúz*), all wrinkled, full of craft and cunning and who, weaving insidious intrigues, catches creatures in the mesh of her snare; lending herself to all and giving herself to none, "an old woman with a thousand lovers" (*'ajuz-i hazár dâmád*). In short, the world is a piece of wizardry, a trick of the conjuror and the illusionist (*shu'bada*). And the more the abyss of the world is revealed to the poet, the more burning becomes his desire to escape from it, and the more raging his thirst to return to his original home.

> Where are the tidings of the Union, that I with all my soul may take the leap?
> I am the bird of the Holy places, could I but leap outside the snare of this world.

This desire for transcendence is at times so irresistible, his ardor so overflowing, that Háfiz not only wants to shatter the glass of confinement, to break down the walls of all the prisons, but goes so far as to overstep the frontiers of the resurrection itself, now too narrow to contain the super abundant ecstasy of a soul who wants to break the cosmic egg, to rend the ceiling of the celestial sphere, "in order to lay there the foundations of a new building."

III. THE PARADOXICAL ETHOS OF THE INSPIRED LIBERTINE

Now what is the ethical behavior of the possessor of the cup of Jam? It is here that the notion of *rend* comes in, that untranslatable term that we render indifferently by "inspired libertine," while taking care to underline the inadequacy of this translation. "The most untranslatable words," says Charles du Bos, "are those that mean most." The word *rend*, as Háfiz understands it, sums up the complex and unique traits of the psychology of the Persian. If, in the words of Berdyaev, Dostoevsky illustrates more than any other Russian thinker the "metaphysical hysteria" of the Russian soul, the *rend* of Háfiz is the most evocative symbol of the indefinable ambiguity of the Persian character, an ambiguity that often confuses not only westerners but also the other peoples of the Orient. The term is pliable, because of its polyvalent cultural content, to interpretations on many levels, which are often contradictory, indeed paradoxical, all the more so because it implicitly contains its ugly side. These conflicting senses are always resolved when they are reintegrated into the initial constellations to which they all belong.

In this term we find the differing tendencies of the Persian character: its suppleness, its power of adaptation which is not necessarily opportunism, but an art of balance and of "shrinking," as Confucius so aptly put it. However, detached from its original sense, this word can come to mean opportunism. This term also evokes all lively lucidity, a savoir faire, refinement of action, tact that goes all the way to compliance, and discretion in speech, which are neither craft nor hypocrisy, nor an affectation of mystery, but can, outside their context, become those very things, being reduced to insidious shifts, not to say to dissembling and imposture. Again, this term denotes an interior liberty, an authentic detachment from the things of this world, suggesting the deliverance, in however small a measure, of the man who lays himself open without shame, naked to the mirror of the world, degenerated from its primitive context, this attitude can turn into one of exhibitionism, of posing and mere libertinism. Equally in this concept we find a sense of immoderacy, a behavior out of the ordinary, shocking, scandalous.

This term expresses, further, a predilection for the uncertain, for language that is veiled and masked, for hints and insinuations, which in the authentic *rend* are expressed in inspired paradoxes (*shathiyát*), in the discipline of the arcane (*taqíya*); but deflected away from its original meaning, it ends in thunderous, puffed-up discourses, and at times in plain falsehood. Finally, there is in this concept a boundless love of the divine such as we see in the great thinkers and mystics of Iranian spirituality. But detached from its mystical content, it is transformed into fanaticism and steered by *homines magni*, to the psychology of the mob. These are the positive qualities of this whole ethic of conduct, almost indecipherable for the non-Persian, with the exception of perhaps the Chinese, that we find in Háfiz's concept of *rend*.

The *rend*, annihilated in the Essence and attaining to subsistence in God, is reborn at the level of the first events and rediscovers the world with the eye with which the Hidden Treasure, unveiling itself, brings to light the magical play of its Beauty. This disinterested gaze, which is also the gaze of the Divine itself, Háfiz calls *nazarbáz*; a term every bit as difficult to translate as the word *rend* itself. Translated literally gives, "he who plays with his gaze." In defining his own vision Háfiz adds:

> I am the lover (*'ashiq*), the *rend*, the *nazarbáz*, I own it in all candor,
> That you may know the manifold arts with which I am adorned.

These multiple arts have a common denominator, which is the *art par excellence* of the one possessed of cosmic vision, but they nevertheless express the various modalities of an extremely subtly-shaded truth. Seen from the perspective of dialectic Love, this art is the art of the lover in quest of union with the Beloved. Considered from the point of view of ethical conduct it will be simply the art of the inspired libertine, whose provocative, scandalous attitude shocks the narrow-minded, breaking the barren charm of conformity with which people called "rational" hem themselves in. And as seen by the interpreter of the "science of the gaze" (*'ilm-i-nazar*), this art will be the magical art of the one who is possessed of the art of the gaze "(*sáhib-i nazar*).

> If the divine face becomes the epiphany of your gaze,
> There is no doubt that now you are possessed of the gaze.

To play with one's gaze means not to apprehend the world as an object or idea, but as an unveiling. Not to see the world as object is also not to represent it as something out there, laid out in front of us, but to discover it as something opening spontaneously, suddenly before us, like the unveiling within ourselves of a flower in blossom. If the *nazarbáz* knows and sees that this unfolding is a Play of the divine gaze, it is because his gaze is a Play which has for stake the play for which the Treasure puts forth its bewitching spell. "It is upon the magical Play of thy gaze," says Háfiz, "that we laid the foundation for our being." Now, to be co-witness of the magical play of the divine gaze is also to free oneself from the hold of the two worlds.

> I say it in all candor and am pleased with what I say,
> Being the slave of Love, I am freed from the two worlds.

It is the union, or the annihilating experience in the Majesty of the essence, and subsistence in its Attributes, which permits the poet to reach the level of the Play, and to be co-witness of the space where this Play unveils itself. It is because of this effacement in this eruption out of the cycle of Being that the poet, tying again the two extremities of the two arcs, in the configuration projected by his gaze, reflects back as the point of coincidence, recomposing and founding again the center and circumference and the pivot which support the axis of the world and the space where the Play of the world opens up. This co-witnessing of the space of the Play is possible only through a surrender of the will, an abandonment to the Play of the divine magic, seeing that it is on the very gratuitousness of this Play that the poet has founded the edifice of his being, and has totally abandoned himself to it.

> On the circle of Destiny we are the point of surrender,
> That your thought may be all grace, your beginning all order.

If the surrender is an unreserved abandonment to the Play and to the space where this Play unveils itself, it is also on the plane of consciousness a non-thought, a stripping away of all that is other than the Divine thought, and on the plane of the will, a non-willing: that is to say, an emptying of all volition which would oppose itself to the bounteous freedom of this Play.

> The thought and will of the self have no existence in our vision
> [the vision of the *rends*];
> The vision and will of selfhood are sacrilege in our religion.

It is armed now with this ethic of non-willing, and supplied with the vision of non-thought, which together constitute the true religion of the *rends*, that Háfiz so relentlessly unlooses himself with a rare audacity that makes him one of the greatest protesters in the history of the world against the prohibition-mongers, inquisitors, accusers, preachers, and tradesmen of gnosis, who in the name of symbols devoid of all content, of religion reduced to a commerce in souls, distill the venom of their blindness, who inwardly are as empty as a drum and destitute of all true sorrow. They are precisely the ones who, in making the Qur'an the "snare of hypocrisy" (*dám-i tazwír*), remain outside the religion of love.

> Speak not to the accusers about the mysteries of Love and of
> drunkenness
> Since you suffer no pain why do you want Him to heal you?

It is the authenticity of this suffering which binds human beings to the root of Being, which is lacking in the inconscient (*bí-khabar*), the rationalists (*'áqil*), the false ascetics, the sanctimonious (*záhid*), whose inauthenticity Háfiz deplores:

> The inconscient are dumbfounded by the play of our gaze.
> I am as I appear; it is for them to play their role.
> The rationalists are the [fixed] point of the compass of Being,
> But Love knows well that their head turns round within this circle.

The inauthenticity of the "inconscient" is not limited solely to certain individuals but represents an entire category of people who, because they take pleasure in the narrow framework of their "selfhood vision" and believe themselves to be the center of the compass of being, do not know that they are drawn along on it by the whirlwind of Love. In other words, they do not know it is Love that turns the circle, and so they remain outside that religion of love whose champion Háfiz became, pushing to its extreme consequences a dispute as old as the world, a dispute which has from time immemorial, and particularly in Persian literature, set in opposition the tolerant generosity of the liberated thinkers and the obsessional meanness of those who think they possess the truth. Háfiz exposes not only a narrow spirit that he styles the narcissistic selfhood-vision. It is not only a reductionist ethic that he denounces as a snare of hypocrisy, but above all a fiction which consists of taking desires for reality.

> Lord forgive the warring of the seventy-two nations,
> For not having seen the truth they have steeped themselves in a fiction

Fiction (*afsána*) is precisely that screen of prejudices and fixed views which the inconscient project upon the unfathomable depth of what at the deepest level remains a disinterested play of the world: in short, all the deceptive appearances which make inauthenticity into a solemn act of self-justification.

In contrast to this, the paradoxical attitude of the *rend* conveys on the ethical, human plane a truth which suffers no limit, no constraint upon others and upon the censor himself, indeed it is the dark side of that which, driven back, reappears showing its other face:

> Those preachers who from the height of their pulpits sparkle in their sermons,
> When back at home devote themselves to business of a different sort.
> I have a difficulty, and submit it to the wise men of this assembly:
> Those who exhort to penitence, why aren't they penitents themselves?
> One would say that no longer believing in the day of the last judgment,
> They corrupt, by their fraud, the work of the supreme Judge.

To corrupt the work of the supreme Judge is to interfere in the natural course of things; it is to judge men, and to curtail the free spontaneity of human beings. For is it not in them that the universality of the divine Names and Attributes is manifested? Who then, Háfiz asks us, could "discern good from evil behind the veil of (multiplicity)?" Sin is for the poet never moral vice: it is instead every constraint that encourages falsity, every fetter which would close an interior door, which would level one of the many dimensions of this mystery that is us; which would lead to the trap, to the futility of empty reputation, to the suffocating limits of an idea, to the absence in life of the suffering of Love, to the sclerosis of everyday life. In short, all that could cause us to remain outside that religion of love, that original religion that we receive as the "heritage of our primordial nature" (*miáath-i fitrat*). Sin is, in the final reckoning, every action that would betray this primordial nature, which would be false to it, and would thwart the spontaneous flowering its Play.

> Though on all sides I am drowned in the sea of sin,
> Being Love's initiate, I am a guest in the house of Mercy.

Let us take an actual example, the closing down of the taverns and the cabarets. This is a so-called hygienic measure which right-minded censors willingly permit themselves in order to reduce sinners to an arid and austere regime of penitence. But this measure has for Háfiz a two-fold baneful consequence: it is, on the one hand, the closing of a door and, considering the quality of the person who instigates it, the closing of an interior dimension, reduced now to the "selfhood vision" of the censor's own narrowness of heart. On the other hand, this closing necessarily coincides with the opening of another door, which is that of falsity, of deceit, of hypocrisy. Háfiz says in this regard:

> If only the doors of the taverns could be reopened again,
> If only the knots of their repressive measures could be untied.
> If by the blind conceit of the pious they are shut,
> Be patient, for thanks to the love of God they will be opened again.
> By the purity of the *rends*, these dawn drinkers,
> Numberless doors will be opened by the key of prayers.
> They are closing the doors of the taverns, O my God do not give your approval,
> For it is the door of hypocrisy they are opening.

The act as such has no absolute value for Háfiz; even blasphemy and sacrilege change their sense according to whether they are envisaged from the point of view of the cosmic vision for the wise person, or from the point of view of the limiting blinkers of the bigots who only project the screen of their own unwillingness. That is to say that every action is bad only if it is grounded in a narrow mind, captive in the nets of the fiction of the world. To the visionary gaze of the *rend*, who is free from all attachment, of all alienating thought, whose heart is polished like a mirror, and who has made his ablutions, like Háfiz himself, in the shining spring of Love, wine, for example, not only is not defiling is rather the elixir of deliverance. And it is in the purple substance of this purifying drink that the poet soaks his prayer-mat. For every inwardly pure being longs for the Friend, it little matters whether he is a sinner or a virtuous man, one who drinks to the dregs, a drunkard or one awakened. And it is also from this original purity that Háfiz's tolerance flows: a tolerance which is not to be taken in the usual sense in which we use this word, but which is a deliverance so fundamental, so original, so far removed from the taints and defilements of prejudices, of beliefs, of confessions and of sects, that it appears as a cleansing spring, obliterating at last all the chimeras that men make for themselves.

And I shall leave the last word to the poet of Shiraz himself:

> Do not judge the *rends*, you who boast your purity—
> No one will indict you for the faults of others.
> What is it to you whether I am virtuous or a sinner? Busy
>   yourself with yourself!
> Each in the end will reap the seed he himself has sown.
> Every man longs for the Friend, the drunkard as much as the
>   awakened.
> Every place is the House of Love, the Synagogue as much as the
>   Mosque.

NOTES TO THE GHAZALS

These notes are numbered according to the *bayt* (English couplet) to which the annotation refers. Metrical patterns here should be read from left to right (while the lines whose scansion they reflect are read right to left).

GHAZAL 1
Meter: o--- o--- o--- o---
       Hazaj muthamman sálim

This is the opening ghazal of Háfiz's *Díwán*. It draws on much of the imagery found in the classical Arabic *qasída*, in which the poet remembers his beloved who has moved away from her campsite, and whom he seeks forever afterwards in the desert wilderness. For an introduction to the *qasída* form and some beautiful translations, see Sells, *Desert Tracings* (1989).

The first and last *misra'* are in Arabic.

Once again, the reader must bear in mind that Persian pronouns do not indicate or express gender. In *bayt*s 4 and 7 the translation could indicate a masculine beloved. See Translators' Introduction, xxiv-xxvii, and notes.

Bayt
1   *sáqí*. The cupbearer, usually a beautiful boy or young man, who brings wine to those in tavern (see Translators' Introduction); also the elusive friend or beloved; a Magian boy (see below); a beautiful and distracting idol.
2   *náfeh*, the scent-pod of the graceful musk deer of central and

southern Asia, the scent of which draws and guides the lover in his search through the desert.

3   *pír-i mughán*, the elder or master of the Magi, Zoroastrian fire-worshippers and thus, in Islamic terms, unbelievers. Unconstrained by the Islamic prohibition against alcohol, Zoroastrians (and Christians) ran the taverns, and the Magus was the tavern-master, the dispenser of wine (with all of its heretical and spiritually symbolic associations). See Translators' Introduction, xxvi-xxvii.

The Magus is also a *pír* or *shaykh*, a spiritual master, who guides his disciples along the states and stations of the mystical path (see notes to Ghazal 4), with which he is intimately familiar. His guidance and instructions must be followed absolutely, even if they appear outwardly to be in contravention of religious law.

Literal translation of the second *misra'*: "for such a traveler is not ignorant of the road and its stopping-places/stations."

4   The transient stopping-place that is the caravanserai also suggests the material world in which we live, and in which we seek pleasure and security.

6   The mystics' secret is the joy of union with God, and this is what is spoken of, or recollected (see *dhikr*, notes to Ghazal 26), in mystic assemblies. Such a joyous secret is hard to keep. The error of the great mystic Halláj was to reveal this secret (see notes to Ghazal 33).

7   Literal translation of the first *misra'*: "If you desire (his/her) presence/attention, never be absent/fall into oblivion, Háfiz."

ghaybat and *hudúr*, the opposites "absence" and "presence," are states encountered on the mystical path: if one seeks the presence of God, one must be absent from oneself. (See Schimmel, *Mystical Dimensions of Islam*, 129 et ff., for additional discussion of such paired states).

GHAZAL 2

Meter: o-o- oo—o-o- oo-
Mujtathth makhbún mahdhúf

Bayt

2   *rind*. rend. See Daryush Shayegan's Afterword, "The Visionary Topography of Háfiz," p. 180 et ff, and Translators' Introduction, xxvi.

> *rabáb*, rebab, a stringed instrument used to accompany a lyric or song.

3 *khirqa*, a patched frock or coat, usually of dark blue wool, which a *pír* bestows upon one who has performed preliminary service and now formally enters on the mystical path. (See notes to Ghazal 4 for a discussion of Háfiz's view of *khirqa*-wearing Sufis and other followers of the mystical path.)

> *deyr-i mughán*, the monastery of the Magi, the tavern (see notes to Ghazal 1).

6 *síb-i zanakhdán*, literally the "apple of the chin," which often has a dimple (*cháh*, literally "well") in the center of it; a source of beauty, and hence distraction, to the lover.

7 *kuhl*, kohl, the black powder placed around the eyes of children and others, thought to improve vision. It is said that the prophet used it to improve his sight.

> Throughout his *Díwán*, Háfiz uses *má* (we) and *man* (I) interchangeably. We have made our choices depending on context.

8 *sabr*, one of the stations of the mystical path, is patience in the face of affliction, patience to accept God's will in whatever form it manifests itself. *Saburí*, an advanced form of *sabr*, is patience under any and all circumstances.

GHAZAL 3

Meter: o-o- oo-- o-o- --
Mujtathth makhbún aslam

Bayt

1 *sabá*, the wind of dawn, traditionally comes from the east, and is auspicious. It brings news, or the scent, of the beloved; it opens rose buds; it relays the lover's love to his beloved and vice versa.

> In the romantic epic poem by Nizámí (1141-1209 CE), *Layla and Majnún*, the poet Qays, forbidden by her father to marry his beloved Layla, goes mad (*majnún*), wandering through the mountains and deserts singing.

2 Parrots were considered intelligent because of their facility with speech and were thought to love sugar because their talk is so sweet. "Sugar-eating parrot" may describe a talented poet, and here in this *bayt* describes the lover, seeking sugar from his beloved.

4   The rose and nightingale are a classic pair of lovers in Persian and other poetry of the Islamic world. The nightingale, as lover, always seeks love from the source of eternal beauty, the rose.

6   The moon is a classic image in Persian poetry, suggesting the face of the beloved (which is pure beauty).

8   *samá',* literally "song" or "hearing," has come to mean the ritual, usually collective, singing of ghazals and other mystical verses. It has gradually acquired the meaning of not only listening but dancing, and can refer to the ecstatic dance practiced by some Sufi orders and condemned by the more orthodox. The dance of the "Whirling Dervishes" of the Mevlevi order in Konya, Turkey, is the example of this form of *samá'* most familiar in the West.

    zuhra, the planet Venus, heaven's musician (see note to Ghazal 27).

    masíh, Jesus, the Messiah, one of the major prophets of Islam. The breath of the *masíh* is the breath of life and can raise the dead as Jesus did Lazarus. See note to Ghazal 24.

GHAZAL 4

Meter: --o -o-o o—o -o-

Mudari' akhrab makfúf mahdhúf

Bayt

1 & 2   As a rule, "Sufi" in Háfiz's *Díwán,* does not carry a positive connotation. While he uses *'árif* and *darwísh* to describe true seekers of the mystical path, by the late fourteenth century many viewed the structured Sufi orders, *taríqahs,* as worldly organizations operating beneath a veneer of spirituality. In these *bayts* Háfiz strikes a contrast between the rend (a true seeker) and the cleric or ascetic (*záhid*) who wears only the external trappings of piety.

    biyá, literally "come," also carries the sense of "look here," "behold," "bring," "agree with me that," "meditate on the fact that." Now that the mirror of the cup's surface is pure and clear, it reflects not only the world (like the cup of Jamshid, see notes to Ghazal 22) but the image of the viewer as an image of the divine.

2   *hál* (pl. *ahwál*), state. The mystical path has both states and stations (*maqám,* pl. *maqámat*). A disciple, through his (or her) own

striving and with appropriate guidance, reaches different stations (stages, "stopping-places") as he proceeds along the path. States come to, and depart from, the disciple's heart by God's will, independent of the disciple's efforts. Some of these states and stations are described in later notes, and a comprehensive discussion of the path and its states and stations can be found in Schimmel, *Mystical Dimensions of Islam*, 98 et ff.

3   The *'anqá*, or Simurgh, is a mythical bird, known by name but not by sight, that lives in Mt. Qáf, the mountain that encircles the world.

4   Adam, the first man and an emblem for mankind, was persuaded by Satan that if he ate of the Tree he would have eternal life. As a result, God forced him to leave the garden with its cool water sources (Suras 20:120 and 2:30).

8   *muríd*, a novice or disciple that has chosen to follow the mystical path under the guidance of a *pír* (see notes to Ghazal 1).

sabá, the dawn wind (see notes to Ghazal 3).

Jám is located in the large province of Khurasan, now in northeastern Iran. The Shaikh to whom Háfiz refers is probably Shaykh Zindeh Pil (1063-1141), who was known for his preaching against, and severe condemnation of, the drinking of wine. "*jám*" can also mean "a cup [of wine]," so this *bayt* could also be read as "take my devotion to the elder of the cup."

GHAZAL 5

Meter: -o—oo—oo-- --
Ramal sálim makhbún mahdhúf

Bayt

4   Literal translation: "O you who draw a polo mallet of pure ambergris across the beautiful moonface/do not upset me, the disoriented one (any further)." In this *bayt* the curved end of the polo stick is a metaphor for the dark, curled hair that falls across the luminous face of the beloved. The lover, disoriented like the polo ball once it has been struck, begs the beloved not to make matters worse.

6   The soil that Noah carried on the ark was the soil or clay from which God had made Adam.

9   Joseph was the beloved lost son of Jacob, the Elder of Canaan.

GHAZAL 6
Meter: --o o--o o--o o--
Hazaj akhrab makhfúf mahdhúf

Bayt

9   Literal translation of this *bayt*: "O palace of the heart-igniter (an epithet for one who sets hearts alight), that is the dwelling-place of intimacy,/May God ensure that the calamity/adversity of time will not destroy you."

GHAZAL 7
Meter: -o—oo—oo-- --
Ramal sálim makhbún mahdhúf

Bayt

1   *rúz-i alast* (see notes to Ghazal 35).
2   The literal translation of the second *misrá'* is: "I said four *takbírs* for everything that exists." *takbír zadan* means to say "Allahu Akbar." Four *takbírs* are required at the end of the funeral rites for a person who has died.
4   Our sense of this *bayt* is that "there," in God's presence and with His grace, there will be no difference between the enormous mountain and the tiny ant, just as there will be no difference between, for example, the portly mullah and the drunken rend.
7   Solomon, who tamed and could ride on the wind, was the wealthiest and most powerful of kings.

GHAZAL 8
Meter: o-o- o-- o-o- oo-
Mujtathth makhbún mahdhúf

Bayt

7   In Islam, blood is considered impure. Having stained the cloister with one pollutant (blood), you have the religious obligation to wash me with another (wine).

8   In Zoroastrian temples, the fire is never allowed to be extinguished.

GHAZAL 9
Meter: --o -o-o o—o -o-
Mudári' akhrab makfúf mahdhúf

Bayt
1   Wine has a rich array of meanings and resonances in Persian poetry, and is associated with light, illumination, and truth. The tilted wineglass can suggest sunrise to the drinker, and the sun itself takes light from the wine. The surface of the wine in the wine cup reveals the face of the beloved, the reflection of one's own face (which, as His creation, is thus a mirror image of God), and, if the cup is Jamshid's (see notes to Ghazal 22), can reveal the world itself.
3   The *sarw* or cypress tree is an image of the tall, graceful, and elegant stature of the beloved. The *sanawbar* or fir tree is used in the same way, but less frequently.
5   Literal translation: "I fear that on the Day of Resurrection the religiously lawful (*halál*) bread of the shaikh will carry no more advantage than our religiously forbidden (*harám*) water (= wine)."
6   The initial *misrá'* can be read two ways: (1) "To the eye of our witness-to-beauty (i.e. the beloved) drunkenness is good/pleasing" or (2) "the drunkenness that comes (to me) because of/from the eye of the witness-to beauty is good."
10   Probably Qavám ud-Dín Hasan (d. 1353), vizier to Abú Isháq Injú, one of Háfiz's early patrons. In his work Háfiz refers several times to Qavam ud-Dín, vizier to Shah Shujá', comparing him to Ásaf, Solomon's advisor and commander. (See notes to Ghazal 15.) During the reign of Mubariz al-Dín Muhammad, Shah Shujá's father, Qavam ud-Dín held a number of powerful positions, including Regent, General, and Governor of Kerman. Threatened by his vizier's influence and authority, Shah Shujá' had Qavam ud-Dín executed in 1362, and Háfiz was devastated.

GHAZAL 10
Meter: -o-- oo—oo-- oo-/--
Ramal sálim makhbún mahdhúf

Bayt

1 *sahar* means first light, not the moment of sunrise.

'ayyár (pl. *'ayyárán*) has no exact equivalent in English. It can describe someone who is nimble and intelligent, who moves quickly here and there, who is something of a vagabond, and sometimes a bandit, trickster, or charlatan.

2 According to tradition, the *wádí* of *ayman* (the right-hand side), or of *íman* (safe, secure), is the riverbed in Sinai where God called to Moses (Suras 20:12 and 70:16).

3 In the second *misra'* the word that Háfiz uses for "tavern" is *kharábát* (literally "house of ruin"), which has the same root as the word "ruin" (*kharáb*) in the first *misra'*.

4 *ishárat*, sign, omen, or allusion to mystical truths.

6 Insane people were often chained. Here the word for "chains," *silsilah*, is an image for the beloved's enchanting hair, and also carries with it the sense of bonds or linkages: lover to beloved, successions of *pírs* in the lineage of a religious order, a strong chain of traditions extending back to the Qur'an and God.

GHAZAL 11
Meter: --o -o-o o—o -o-
Mudárí akhrab makfúf mahdhúf

Bayt

4 *karím*, The Generous, is one of the attributes and Divine Names of God.

9, 10 The *mudda'í*, the false lover or impostor, does not understand true love, has not suffered its pain, and composes his verses for self-advancement. (See Translators' Introduction p. xxvi, and Meisami, *Medieval Persian Court Poetry*, 268, 296.)

GHAZAL 12
Meter: o-o- oo-- o-o- oo-/--
Mujtathth makhbún maqsúr

Bayt

2 *himma*, "high spiritual energy/ambition," is the spiritual power

that enables an adept to attain higher planes of experience and understanding, and that enables the *pír* to protect his disciples.

3   *surúsh*, is the angel of inspiration, a messenger, and a guide to poets, sometimes synonymous with Gabriel. Here the voice is the contact, the aural connection, with the invisible world.

4   *sháhbáz*, royal falcon, often an image for man, God's favorite falcon, who longs to be called home, just as a hunting falcon is called back to the prince's wrist with a drum.

6   *pír-i taríqat*, master of the *taríqat*, the spiritual path or road traveled by the disciple, that branches off the wider thoroughfare of Islamic law (*sharí'a*). See Schimmel, *Mystical Dimensions*, 98.

GHAZAL 13
Meter: o-o- oo—o-o- oo-/--
Mujtathth makhbún maqsúr

Bayt

1   *khálí az khalal* means "empty of/without flaw or impurity," without the type of flaw that one finds in a precious stone, or the type of impurity that one finds in a wine.

2   *'áfíyat*, literally "health," but here in the spiritual sense. This *bayt* might refer to the Islamic *pul-i sarát* which aligns with the Zoroastrian *pul-i chínevad*, a very narrow bridge which you have to cross, and if you fail you fall into hell.

3   Literal translation of this *bayt*: "I am not the only one in the world who is afflicted from lack of practice, the affliction of the *'ulemá* is also knowledge/learning without practice." That is, they have knowledge but do not act on it.

6   The curls, or tresses, are chains that bind the lover, but by analogy also link one to God. See notes to Ghazal 10.

       Zuhra, Venus is considered an auspicious planet (see notes to Ghazal 27). *Zuhal*, Saturn, the black planet, is considered highly inauspicious.

7   *azal*, "pre-eternity," is the period before Creation, before God's primordial covenant with man. See Shayegan's Afterword, p. 171 et ff.

GHAZAL 14

Meter: -o-- oo-- oo-- oo-/--
Ramal sálim makhbún mahdhúf

Bayt

2 *nargis*, the narcissus, hangs its head and suggests the languid, sultry, or perhaps intoxicated eyes of the beloved. It is often used to mean simply "eyes."

3 *díríneh*, "ancient," does not refer to the age of the addressee, but means "of old," from a long time ago.

7 *tauba*, a vow of repentance that must be serious and eternal in order to be acknowledged and accepted by God; also the name of the initial station of the mystical path, in which one repents and turns away from the snare that is the world in order to seek a higher reality.

GHAZAL 15

Meter: -o-- oo-- oo-- oo-/--
Ramal sálim makhbún mahdhúf

Bayt

2 *tilismát*, talismans, here can also mean magic formulae, or spells.

3 Literal translation of the first *misrá*: "The palace of paradise, to which Rizwán went to be its doorkeeper..." Rizwán is the gatekeeper of heaven.
suhbat, "society, friendship, conversation, companionship" implies great intimacy here.

7 *qibla*, the direction of prayer; in Islam, the Ka'ba in Mecca toward which all Muslims direct the recital of their canonical prayers, and with which all mosques are aligned.

9 *az azal tá be-ábad*, "from before pre-eternity/creation until eternity-without-end" See Shayegan's Afterword, p. 171 et ff.

10 *himma*, spiritual power (see notes to Ghazal 12).

11 Qárún, like Croesus, had treasures "such that the very keys of them were too heavy a burden for a company of men endowed with strength" (Sura 28:76). Qárún exulted in his wealth, believing that his own wisdom, rather than God's will, was the source

of his good fortune. God had the earth swallow Qárún beneath the weight of his possessions. For a discussion of *gheyrat*, here translated as "wrath," see notes to Ghazal 20.

13   Ásaf ibn Bakhíya, vizier to Solomon, was viewed as a wise and model statesman. Here the reference probably refers to one of two of Háfiz's patrons, both referred to elsewhere as Ásaf Tháni: Qavám ud-Dín Muhammad Sáhib-i 'Ayar, or Khwajah Jalál ud-Dín Tauransháh, both viziers to Shah Shujá'.

GHAZAL 16
Meter: -o-- oo-- oo-- oo-/--
Ramal sálim makhbún mahdhúf

Bayt

1   *but* (pl. *bután*), "idol" carries with it most of its English connotations (including the religious condemnation of idolaters as unbelievers), but usually refers to the beloved, or to a person of great, and thus distracting, sensual beauty.
dín can mean not only "religion" or "faith," but also more broadly "way of life."

5   *faqr*, "poverty," the quality of being unattached to material things, is a source of spiritual wealth, and a central aim and concern to those setting out on, and traveling along, the mystical path.

6   The *shahnih* is a watchman or policeman, on the lookout for those deviating from orthodox behavior.
   In the second *misrá'*, Háfiz uses the word *sultán*, which means "king," creating a nice contrast to the constable in the first *misrá'*. In this context, *sultán* can also refer to God.

7   The Ka'ba (see also notes to Ghazal 15) is the shrine of black stone in the Great Mosque at Mecca. It is the endpoint of the great pilgrimage of the Hajj. Read figuratively here it can also mean "the ultimate goal."

8   Khusrau Parvíz was the last great Sassanian king, whose story was well-known from Firdawsi's epic *Sháhnámeh*. His love for the Armenian Christian princess Shirin is the topic of Nizámi's *Khusrau and Shirin*. *Khusrau-i shírín* also means "sweet king," creating wordplay in the final *bayt* and probably referring to a patron.

GHAZAL 17

Meter: --o -o-o o—o -o-
Mudári' akhrab makfúf mahdhúf

Bayt

3 Literal translation of the second *misrá'*: "Be the consoler of yourself. What is the pain of/caring about time/fate?"

4 Iram, a city in Yemen where a legendary garden was built by the Arab king Shaddad to duplicate paradise. It was destroyed by a storm sent as a warning against such hubris (Suras 89:6-8 and 34:16). This may also be a reference to a specific garden in Shiraz.

7 According to Shari'a law, a sin committed unintentionally is not considered a sin.

Ámorezgár, a Divine Name of God, means "The All-Forgiving."

8 *záhid*, ascetic (see notes to Ghazal 4). Kawthar is one of the fountains or ponds in paradise.

GHAZAL 18

Meter: -o-- -o-- -o-- -o-
Ramal mahdhúf

Bayt

2 "Straight/righteous road" incorporates into the *misrá'* a phrase from the *fátiha*, the opening Sura of the Qur'an (Sura 1:6). The Sura is part of the daily prayers:

>In the name of God
>The Compassionate the Caring
>Praise be to God
>lord sustainer of the worlds
>the Compassionate the Caring
>master of the day of reckoning
>To you we turn to worship
>and to you we turn in time of need
>Guide us along the road straight
>the road of those to whom you are giving
>not those with anger upon them

not those who have lost the way.

Translation, with supporting discussion, in Michael Sells, *Approaching the Qur'an* (Ashland, OR: White Cloud Press, 1999), 42.

6   In the corner of governmental decrees there was usually a small seal or calligraphed phrase (*toghrá*) affirming that everything, including the things ordered in the decree, were subject to God's will. The implication here is that government officials, in their arrogance, have forgotten that fact.

GHAZAL 19
Meter: --o -o-o o—o -o-
Mudári' akhrab makfúf mahdhúf

Bayt
1   *ján sipárdan*, "to entrust one's soul" also means "to give up one's life."
2   *istikhárah*, divination or prognostication, usually to ascertain whether something is auspicious or inauspicious by letting a Qur'an fall open and reading the page, or by taking a random segment of prayer beads and counting them out. Háfiz's *Díwán* is also used for divination in this manner.
3   According to a *hadith qudsí*, a tradition or saying which came directly from God but is not found in the Qur'an, God said, "I was a hidden treasure, and I loved to be known, so I created the world." See Shayegan's Afterword, p. 170–171.
4   *wiláyat*, "province, dominion, territory" can also mean "saintship, holiness, sanctity," a quality possessed by accomplished mystics.
5   *máh párih*, the beautiful one, literally means "sliver/piece of moon."
6   In Persian short vowels are not written. Depending on whether the short vowel here is "i" or "u," the verb here can mean either "pulling" (*kishad*) or "killing" (*kushad*), and is meant to suggest both.

GHAZAL 20
Meter: -o-- oo-- oo-- oo-/--
Ramal sálim makhbún mahdhúf

Bayt

1   *kawn-o makán*, literally "existence/creation" and "place/locality" denotes the created universe, physical reality.

3   The *sidra* and the *túbá* are tall shade trees in paradise.

4   All of the ascetic's visible efforts to attain heaven's garden will prove useless.

6   *faná*, meaning death or annihilation, is also a technical term in the mystical lexicon. In such a context "annihilation" describes the mystic's goal: it is the reverse of coming-into-being or becoming and represents the (re)absorption of the mystic into the Divine Essence. This is not a union of two separate entities, but a return to man's pre-creation state, when he was in God. The moth, when it burns upon achieving union with the flame it seeks, experiences *faná*.

7   *gheyrat*, a term that has no equivalent in English, means sometimes "jealousy or possessiveness," "zeal," "wrath," "ardor," or "intense energy or enthusiasm." Here, Háfiz cautions the ascetic not to become too complacent or smug in his charade of zealousness, as God can tell the difference between false and true spiritual zeal.

GHAZAL 21

Meter: -o-- oo-- oo-- oo-/--
Ramal sálim makhbún mahdhúf

Bayt

1-2   These two *bayts* echo lines from several Suras of the Qur'an: "Every soul earns only to its own account; no soul bears the load of another." (Sura 6:164), "Whosoever is guided, is only guided to his own gain, and whosoever goes astray, it is only to his own loss; no soul laden bears the load of another." (Sura 17:15), and similar passages in Suras 35:18 and 5:105. (Trans. A. J. Arberry, *The Koran Interpreted*. New York: Macmillan, 1955.)

4   A *khesht* is an uncooked mud brick. In this *bayt* there are two such bricks, one in each *misrá*': the first is that which makes up the threshold at the doorway of the tavern, the second is the brick that is placed at one end of a grave so that the corpse will have a place to lay its head.

5   The primordial covenant between God and man, made in *azal*, the time before creation. See Shayegan's Afterword, p 174 et ff.
6   "My/Our father" here refers to Adam, who was expelled from Eden.
7   We read this *bayt*, like the ones above it, as addressed to the "holier-than-thou" ascetic of the opening *bayt*.
8   The word for tavern here is *kharábát*, literally "house of ruin," chosen as a fitting contrast to "heaven."

GHAZAL 22
Meter: --o -o-o o--o -o-
Mudári' akhrab makfúf mahdhúf

The imagery throughout this ghazal intertwines the act of loving with the act of making the *hajj*, or pilgrimage to the Sacred Enclosure and Ka'ba at Mecca.

Bayt
2, 6   *harám*, sanctuary, sacred enclosure. *harím-i harám*, "holiest of/sanctuary of sanctuaries," refers usually to the precincts of Mecca and Medina. It can also be understood as proximity to the beloved.
3   *bakht*, "luck" can mean any kind of luck, good or bad, and thus is similar to, although less weighty than, "fate" or "destiny."
5   *muhtasib*, the equivalent of a religious policeman or enforcer, who makes his rounds of the city to ensure that the provisions of the Shari'a law (such as those against drinking alcohol) are being obeyed.
    Jamshid, one of the first mythical kings of Persia, is found in the *Sháhnámeh* of Ferdowsi. He possessed a goblet which revealed the entire world to the person looking into it. Iram (see notes to Ghazal 17) was said to be his seat of power, and his cup was of no help in averting the garden city's destruction by God.
7   *bibar guy*, a term drawn from the game of polo, means "to take/steal the ball" and take it down the field to victory.

GHAZAL 23
Meter: --o -o-o o--o -o-
Ramal sálim makhbún mahdhúf

Bayt

2   *bigardash narasídím*, literally "we did not reach her/his dust," meaning that as the beloved took off, no matter what we did, we couldn't even reach the dust that had been stirred up by her/him and then slowly settled on the road in her/his wake.

3   *fátiha*, the opening sura of the Qur'an; *hirz yamání*, an auspicious prayer which Muhammad supposedly learned from Uways Qaraní, an illiterate, on the road to Yemen; *ikhlás*, Sura 112 of the Qur'an. The first two of these prayers are part of the namáz, the Muslim's ritual prayer, and all are normally addressed to God and to God alone.

GHAZAL 24

Meter: --o -o-o o--o -o-
Mudári' akhrab makfúf mahdhúf

Bayt

2   When a candle begins to sputter, its wick is trimmed with a knife or scissors, after which it burns again with a bright and steady flame.
    Literal translation of the second *misrá'*: "and this very old man began youth (again) from the beginning."

4   *pistih*, a pistachio, conveys the image of a beautiful mouth: tiny, partly-opened lips, smiling.

5   *'isádam*, one who has the breath of the Messiah, Jesus. An *'isádam* can breathe life into inanimate objects, heal the sick, and raise the dead (Sura 5:109), as the beloved can do for the lover. See also notes to Ghazal 3.

7   Literal translation of this *bayt*: "Because of this talk/story the seven domes of heaven are full of clamor./See the short-sighted one who took the tale/talk/verse to be of little importance."

8   *ta'widh*, an amulet, usually consisting of verses from the Qur'an tightly rolled and encased in metal and worn on the person. Verses concerning the *'isádam* are considered exceptionally auspicious.

GHAZAL 25

Meter: --o -o-o o--o -o-
Ramal sálim makhbún mahdhúf

This ghazal is discussed in detail by Julie Meisami in "The Analogical Structure of a Persian Courtly Lyrics" and "The World's Pleasure." *Medieval Persian Court Poetry*, 286-97.

Bayt

3   The pearls and rubies that the tip of the eyelash(es) must pierce are the tears and heart-blood that flow from the lover's eyes.
4   *abad*, eternity-without-end, see notes to Ghazal 15.
5   The rosegarden of Iram, see notes to Ghazal 17.
6   Jamshid, see notes to Ghazal 22. The "throne of Jamshid" is the Persian name for Persepolis, and this throne to which Háfiz speaks may refer also to his patron Abu Isháq.

   A literal translation of the second *misrá'*: "It said, 'Alas, for that waking (i.e. good) fortune/realm has gone to sleep.'"
8   *sabr*, patience, see notes to Ghazal 2.

GHAZAL 26
Meter: --o -o-o o--o -o-
       Mudári' akhrab makfúf mahdhúf

Bayt

1   The wise hoopoe (*hudhud*) was a friend to King Solomon, who could understand the language of birds. It was the hoopoe that first brought Solomon news of the Queen of Sheba (Sura 27:20). In Persian poetry the hoopoe is a go-between, the bird that leads the lover to the beloved. In 'Attár's *Mantiq ut-tayr* (*Conference of the Birds*) it is the hoopoe who leads the other birds in quest of the mythical divine bird, the Simurgh. The hoopoe has the attributes of the dawn wind who brings news of the lover to the beloved and vice versa. The *bayt* can also be read as: "O, dawn wind [who performs the same task as the hoopoe of Solomon] I am sending you as a messenger to the beloved. You have a long way to go and a very important task to perform."
2   A bird is often used as an image or figure for the soul. Here Háfiz may be speaking to his own.
3   *qurb*, "proximity," is one of the stages of the mystical path. It has been explained by 'Alí ibn 'Uthmán al-Hujwírí as "an ethical

proximity, brought forth by the fulfillment of God's orders, the opposite of separation from God caused by man's disobedience." (Cited from *Kashf al-Mahjúb* in Schimmel, *Mystical Dimensions*, 133.)

In the first *misrá'*, Háfiz says that there is no station that is simultaneously near (to the beloved or to God) and far (from the beloved or from God). In the second *misrá*, he says that he can see "you" clearly (implying proximity) but "sends greetings" (implying distance).

4   The east wind and north wind, respectively the winds of morning and evening, are trusted carriers of prayers, messages, and scents. See also notes to Ghazal 3.

8   *qawl*, a short lyric poem or saying which, like the ghazal, is often sung.

10 *dhikr* is the Sufi practice of "recollecting" or "remembering" God. This recollection and the constant repetition of God's names (or other formulae deemed appropriate by the *pír* or *shaikh*) takes many forms, and can be performed silently or aloud, alone or in the company of fellow dervishes, sometimes with music. Like other forms of silent prayer or collective meditation in other religions, *dhikr* is considered a primary tool in developing the adept's spiritual concentration. To ensure that an invited guest would have no excuse for declining an invitation, the host would send the guest a horse and riding coat.

GHAZAL 27
Meter: --o -o-o o--o -o-
Mudári' akhrab makfúf mahdhúf

Bayt

2   Supplicants touch or clasp the hem of the person of whom they are asking assistance.

3   The *mihráb* is the arched prayer-niche in the wall of a mosque, aligned with the Ka'ba of Mecca, towards which one prays, lifting one's arms in prayer.

4   Literal translation: "Even if I must go to Hárút of Babylon [to learn magic/sorcery]..." There are many variants of the tale. The general story is that the angels protested to God that people on

earth were being permitted to sin without adequate punishment. God decided to let the angels try to resist such temptations and sent two powerful angels, Hárút and Marút, to Babylon (Sura 2:101). They became entranced by a beautiful woman, began drinking alcohol and attempted to seduce her. She tricked them into revealing to her the ineffable and greatest name of God, by means of which she turned herself into a star (Venus). In punishment Hárút and Márút were made to hang by their feet inside a well in Mount Damavand, perpetually thirsty but unable to reach the water to drink.

GHAZAL 28
Meter: --o -o-o o--o -o-
Mudári' akhrab makfúf mahdhúf

Bayt
2   The candle's flame is considered its tongue. Here, the enormity and power of the secret incinerates the candle's tongue, preventing it from spilling that secret to the uninitiated.
5   The outer leg of the of compass has freedom to move but the one at the center is fixed. You can range freely until you fall in love, whereupon the beloved becomes your world and you are rooted in the center of it, unable to move.

GHAZAL 29
Meter: o-o- oo—o-o- oo--
Mujtathth makhbún

The wordplay throughout this ghazal is a tour de force. As can be seen in the Persian, the word *guft* ("he/she/it said") appears not only as part of the *radíf* but repeatedly throughout the poem, and four times in the last *bayt*.

Bayt
1   The elder of Canaan is Jacob, father of Joseph.
5   The station of *rezá* is the last and highest stations of the mystical path and it means to surrender to all the adversities of life without any resentment in one's heart.

The *raqíb'*, "chaperone," "rival," "guardian," is the one who protects and guards the beloved and keeps away the lover. In his commentary on Háfiz's *Díwán*, Kazem Bargnaysi reads this *bayt* as: "From now on I will be in the station of *rezá*, or, I have reached that station and will not complain about anything. Therefore, I am thankful to your guardian (who kept me away from you), because my heart, now, is used to the pain of separation and is no longer seeking a remedy." Bargnaysi, 148.

6   In the path of Solomon's advancing army, an ant frantically told all the other ants that they should take shelter so as to not be trampled. Solomon, who had mastered the winds and was advancing with his army through the air, asked the ant why he thought he needed shelter, given that the hooves of his army wouldn't touch the ground. The ant told the great king, "The air is not permanent or reliable, and you and your army could fall to earth any time and crush all of us." *Stories of the Qur'an*, in Khorramshahi, 470.

GHAZAL 30
Meter: --o -o-- --o -o—
Mudári' akhrab sálim

Bayt
6   In the second *misrá'* the literal meaning of "killer" is "blood-spiller," picking up the imagery from the first *misrá'*.
10   The Qur'an was orally transmitted by God to Muhammad, and as he and the original Companions died and the text was transcribed into Arabic, differing versions of the Qur'an developed. In the 9th century CE, it was decided that seven original "readers" would be considered authoritative, and that two transmitted versions of each reader would be considered legitimate. There is little material difference between versions.

GHAZAL 31
Meter: -o-- -o-- -o-
Ramal mahdhúf

Bayt

5   The Zindehrúd, literally "river of life," is the river that flows through Isfahan.

GHAZAL 32

Meter: o--- o--- o--- o---
       Hazaj muthamman sálim

Bayt

1   *khátir*, a "heart/mind" that is *majmú'*. *Majmú'* is a technical term used by mystics to mean spiritually-focused, undistracted by material or worldly things.

2   Literal translation of the second *misrá'*: "the one who kisses that threshold must have his/her life/soul in his/her sleeve (from whence he can scatter it, as he must, like coins)."

3   According to the Qur'an, Solomon had an inscribed seal which gave him power over animals and spirits.

4   *khatt*, means both a line of written script and also the line of a new down moustache that appears on the upper lip of the beloved, here a sensuous boy on the edge of manhood. Because the Persian script does not distinguish short vowels, the *khatt* of the beloved can be read as either "dark" (*mishkín*) or "musk-scented" (*mushkín*).

6   *faqír-i rah-nishín*, "road-sitting pauper." A true *faqír* is one whose life is lived in complete accord with the quality of *faqr* (see notes to Ghazal 16).

7   See the story of the uncharitable farmers who prevented the poor from coming into their garden and were punished by God in the Qur'an (Sura 68:17-33).

8   Legendary kings Kay Khusrau and Jamshid (see notes to Ghazals 16 and 22, respectively).

GHAZAL 33

Meter: oo--/-o-- oo-- oo-- oo-/--
       Ramal sálim makhbún mahdhúf

Bayt

1   Jamshid's cup, see notes to Ghazal 22.

2   The shell of the *kawn-o makán*, the universe. See notes to Ghazal 20.

3   The *pír-i mughán*, the master of the Magi. See notes to Ghazal 1.
    While *dúsh* means literally "last night," it can also refer to *azal*, pre-eternity or the eve of creation. See notes to Ghazal 13.

4   The mirror here suggests both the surface of the world-seeing cup and the heart of the Magus himself. The mystic's task is to constantly polish his or her heart so that it may better reflect God and His manifestations.

5   *hakím*, "the Wise," "the All-Knowing," is one of the names and attributes of God. The word is also used to refer to Greek philosophers or physicians.

6   This *bayt* refers to Husayn ibn Mansúr al-Halláj (857-922), the famous Sufi martyr who came to symbolize the ecstasy, as well as the suffering, of the lover's personal union with God. His fault, according to the Sufi tradition, was that he openly revealed his great secret to the ears of the uninitiated by declaring to the people of Baghdad, "*áná'l haqq*," "I am the Truth (one of the Names of God)," the ultimate expression of complete and undifferentiated union with God. For this heresy against the orthodox, and for political reasons, he was sentenced to death during the reign of Abbasid Caliph al-Muqtadir (908-32) and was, after a lengthy imprisonment, hung and beheaded. He is said to have danced all the way to the gallows.

7   *ahwál*, "states" (*hál*, sing.). Although the word is most often used in the ordinary sense of "state, condition," *hál* is also a technical term in Islamic mysticism. See notes to Ghazal 4.

8   Literal translation of the *bayt*: "All these sleights-of-hand tricks that he (i.e. reason) was doing there [at the creation of Adam] the sorcerer was doing before the rod and white hand [of Moses]." Pharaoh called upon Moses to prove that he was indeed a messenger from God by staging a competition between Moses and the Pharaoh's own sorcerers. Moses cast down his rod, which turned into a serpent and then devoured the serpents magically created by the other sorcerers. He then drew his hand forth from his robes and it glowed with a white light. In the face of these miracles Pharaoh's sorcerers withdrew from the competition (Sura 7:104 ff).

9   *Jesus, the 'isadam,* see notes to Ghazal 24.
10 The dark chains of the idol's (beloved's) hair are both the cause of, and the relief for, Háfiz's love-frenzied heart. They are also a metaphor for the complicated secrets and mysteries of the Path. The idol, *but,* is discussed in the notes to Ghazal 16.

GHAZAL 34
Meter: o-o- oo-- o-o- --
Mujtathth makhbún aslam

Bayt
1   Jamshid, see notes to Ghazal 22.
    kuhl, kohl, see notes to Ghazal 2.
3   The dawn wind serves the rose (the object of its desire), and in response the rose drops the green of its outer bud and reveals its blossom. The lover serves his beloved in this way, as does the disciple his master.
7   *tabi'at,* "nature," meaning the natural functions or temper of person.
    taríqat, the spiritual path, see notes to Ghazal 12.
8   The candle's sputter is its laughter, see notes to Ghazal 24.
10 *haqíqat,* "truth" or "reality," here in the sense of the ultimate spiritual reality.

GHAZAL 35
Meter: oo--/-o-- oo-- oo-- oo-/--
Ramal sálim makhbún mahdhúf

One of the most cryptic of Háfiz's ghazals, this is considered by many to be the finest of them. The discussions in the various commentaries are lengthy, explore in detail various levels of meaning, and are not replicated here.

Bayt
1   *azal,* "pre-eternity," see notes to Ghazal 15.
    tajallí, "manifestation," "revelation," "illumination," "making-visible." The relationship between God and His creatures can be condensed, very roughly, in this way: "The Absolute yearned

in His Loneliness, and according to the tradition 'I was a hidden treasure and I wanted to be known, so I created the world,' produced creation as a mirror for his *tajallíyát*, His manifestations." Schimmel, *Mystical Dimensions of Islam*, 268. See Shayegan, Afterword, p. 171.

2   *gheyrat* has no English equivalent, and blends the qualities of jealousy, possessiveness, anger, intense energy, and zeal. See also notes to Ghazal 20.

On the Day of Alast (see notes to Ghazals 7 and 38) God first offered the burden of His love to the heavens with its angels and heavenly host, to the earth, and then to the mountains. All of them were fearful, and refused to accept it. Adam made the foolish choice to accept it. This trust (*amánat*) defines mankind's special relationship to God (Sura 33:72). Islamic mystics believe that this *amánat* is love.

3   Reason, the enemy of love, seeks to acquire some of love's light. Love will not allow it.

4   Like reason in the *bayt* above, the impostor (*mudda'í*, see notes to Ghazal 11) also wants access to the secret of love, but as he is not an intimate (*mahram*), love sends him packing.

6   *ján 'ulwí*, called also *ruh-i malakúti*. the "celestial or angelic soul," as opposed to one of the lower souls.

GHAZAL 36
Meter: o-o- oo-- o-o- --
         Mujtathth makhbún aslam

Bayt
4   *nargis*, the eyes as a narcissus, see notes to Ghazal 14.
5   Literal translation of the second *misrá'*: "where is the lion-hearted one who does not/will not avoid calamity/affliction?"
6   *sabúrí*, patience, see notes to Ghazal 2.

GHAZAL 37
Meter: -o-- oo-- oo-- oo-/--
         Ramal sálim makhbún mahdhúf

Bayt

1   *mahram-i del,* "intimate of the heart." Islamic mystics believe that the heart is the treasure of divine secrets and the place of the manifestation and beholding of the Truth. Therefore, *mahram-i del* is the true *arif*, the one who has discovered the treasure of secrets in the heart and has reached the stage of seeing. (Bargnaysi, 266.)

3, 4   See notes to Ghazal 4 for a discussion of the way in which Sufis, wearers of the *khirqa* (see notes to Ghazal 2), are viewed by Háfiz. Háfiz distinguishes here between true mystics and those who only wear the external trappings on the mystic.

4   "My story" can mean either (a) the story that Háfiz tells about his love or (b) the story that others tell about Háfiz and his outrageous behaviors.

6   *azal tá bi-abad,* see notes to Ghazal 15.

8   *nargis,* the narcissus, is discussed in notes to Ghazal 14. The phrase *chashm-i bímár* (literally "sick eyes"), means the sultry and languid eyes of the beloved. That the narcissus is trying to mimic the beloved's "sick eyes" sets up wordplay between the two *misrá'*.

9   Hearts and souls were thought to nest in the beloved's hair. See also Ghazal 39.

GHAZAL 38

Meter: -o-- oo-- oo-- oo-/--
Ramal sálim makhbún mahdhúf

Bayt

1   Adam was made from clay kneaded and formed with love by God's own hand, and then given life by God's breath. The angels were commanded by God to bow down to Adam because, unlike the angelic host, part of man's nature is divine (Sura 15:29).

   paymáneh, "cup," creates a nice visual pun, as in Persian *paymán* means "treaty" or "covenant," linking to bayt 3.

3   *amánat,* see notes to Ghazal 35.

4   These are the seventy-two sects of Islam.

   haqíqat: truth, ultimate reality, see also notes to Ghazal 34.

6   According to the Qur'an the downfall of Adam and Eve was by means of a cereal grain, not a piece of fruit.

GHAZAL 39

Meter: o--- o--- o--- o---
Hazaj muthamman sálim

Bayt

2   The second *misrá'* can be read as either "to scatter" or "to sacrifice" the souls of lovers entangled in the beloved's hair.
3   *khátir* means both "heart" and "mind." See notes to Ghazal 32.
7   The martyr Husayn ibn Mansúr al-Halláj, see notes to Ghazal 33.

GHAZAL 40

Meter: -o-- -o-- -o-- -o-
Ramal mahdhúf

Bayt

1   *vá'iz*, the preacher who leads communal prayer in the mosque. The *mihráb* is the niche in the mosque wall to which Muslims pray during communal prayer; the *minbar* is the pulpit from which a preacher delivers his sermon to those assembled in the mosque.
2   *tauba*, repentance, see notes to Ghazal 14.
3   *dávar*, "the Judge," is one of the names or attributes of God.
4   *bí-niyází*, "needlessness," is considered by some to be a station on the mystical path.
8   *khánaqah*, the physical building(s) that house Sufi activities and personnel.
10 Much medieval teaching was done by rote, and the clamor of schoolchildren trying to memorize sections of the Qur'an or other types of verse can still be heard from the streets of the Islamic world.

GHAZAL 41

Meter: -o-- oo-- oo-- oo-/--
Ramal sálim makhbún mahdhúf

Bayt

1, 3   *daftar*, a notebook in which one writes poems or other things. One could also read this as an image of the poet's heart or soul.

	In medieval times one often washed the ink writing from a notebook when what was written was no longer needed, in order to re-use the notebook.
4	In the first *misrá*, *án* means a quality that is difficult to express, "a certain or special something."
	bután, idols, see notes to Ghazal 16.
	dar 'ilm-i nazar can mean (a) in the "science of the gaze"—see Shayegan's Afterword, p 181–182; (b) in the science of crafting intricate and sophisticated verse; or(c) in the science of the study of the *sharía'* or religious law. Háfiz doubtless wants us to savor the irony of all three meanings.
5	A compass (*pargàr*, in the first *misrà'*) has two legs: the one that is fixed (*pà*, "foot") and the one that moves (*sar*, "head). In the second *misrà* Háfiz plays nicely on this in his use for "bewildered" (*sar-gashteh*, "head-turned") and "firm" (*pà bar jà*, "foot in place").
8	"Rose-colored" suggests Háfiz is referring to the tavern-master, whose garments are stained with wine. Dervishes traditionally wore coats of blue wool. For Háfiz's views of the Sufis, see notes to Ghazal 4.
9	There is an untranslatable pun here. *qalb* can mean either "heart" or "counterfeit coin." Háfiz wishes to give the beloved/God his heart, presumably in exchange for union with him/her/Him. But the beloved, like a savvy merchant, can tell that what Háfiz offers is flawed or counterfeit.

GHAZAL 42

Meter: -o-- oo-- oo-- oo-/--
Ramal sálim makhbún mahdhúf

Bayt

2	*azal*, before creation, see notes to Ghazal 15. Slaves wore in their ear a ring which indicated both their slave status and the identity of their master.
3	*himma*, spiritual ambition or power, see notes to Ghazal 12.

GHAZAL 43

Meter: -o-- oo-- oo-- oo-/--
Ramal sálim makhbún mahdhúf

Bayt

3   Jamshid, see notes to Ghazal 22. The seal of Jamshid may be the lips of the beloved; the image of God or of the beloved falls on the ruby bezel of the lover's heart. In Persian literature, especially in Háfiz's poetry, the image of Jamshid and Solomon are often fused. Here the seal of Jamshid is the seal of Solomon that was mentioned before.

4   *shahnih*, watchman, policeman, see notes to Ghazal 16.

GHAZAL 44

Meter: --o -o-- ---o -o--
        Mudári' akhrab sálim

Bayt

1   *agar bar áyad* can mean both "if it comes to pass" and "if it comes up over the horizon."

3   *khayál*, the dream image or phantom image of the beloved that comes at night, or in one's sleep.

GHAZAL 45

Meter: o-o- oo-- o-o- --
        Mujtathth makhbún aslam

Bayt

4   The word for skull means literally "cup of the head (*kasih-ye sar*)." Jamshid, Bahman, and Qobad were ancient legendary and historical pre-Islamic Persian kings. For more on Jamshid and his cup, see notes to Ghazal 22.

5   Keykavus is also an ancient legendary pre-Islamic king and appears in Ferdowsi's *Shahnameh*.

6   Persian legend and the poetic tales of Nizámí say that to win the hand of beautiful Shirin, Farhad the architect performed many tasks, including digging a tunnel through a rocky mountain so the milk of Shirin's cows could reach a lower elevation more easily. King Khusrau, her husband, in love with her himself, sent to Farhad the (false) news that Shirin had died. Upon hearing this, Farhad committed suicide, and in this *bayt* the blood from his

eyes nurtures the tulip, the dark red, cup-shaped flower of suffering. (Schimmel, *Two-Colored Brocade: The Imagery of Persian Poetry*. See also notes to Ghazal 16.)

9   The Musallah gardens in Shiraz are now the site of Háfiz's tomb. The Ruknabad is the river that runs through the city.

GHAZAL 46

Meter: -o-- oo-- oo-- oo-/--
        Ramal sálim makhbún mahdhúf

Commentaries suggest that this ghazal was composed after the death of Qavam al-Dín (see notes to Ghazal 9).

Bayt

1   We read this first *bayt* as addressed, carefully, to Shah Shujá'.
3   Farhad and Shirin, see notes to Ghazal 45.
4   While God gave gold treasure to kings, to beggars he gave "the corner of contentment."

GHAZAL 47

Meter: o-o- oo-- o-o- oo-/--
        Mujtathth makhbún aslam

Bayt

4   Parrots love sugar, see notes to Ghazal 3.

GHAZAL 48

Meter: o--- o--- o---
        Hazaj maqsúr

Bayt

2   In Háfiz's work the parrot is often a metaphor for the pen. This parrot is the one who reveals secrets because it repeats its owner's interior secrets.

The literal translation of the phrase "may you live long" is "may your head be green," which is, of course, the color of the parrot.

3, 6   *harífán* can mean either "companions" or "rivals."

4   A literal translation of the phrase "bright luck" is "awake (good) luck". On luck generally, see notes to Ghazal 22.

       To waken a sleeper, one sprinkles rosewater on their face. Rosewater "from the cup" can here be a reference to wine, which wakes one from unawareness and ignorance.

5   *dar pardah* here can mean that the minstrel played his melody (a) "on the fret (of his instrument)," and/or (b) "within/behind the veil," and/or (c) "within a certain (musical) mode."

7   According to the legends and romances of the time, Alexander the Great of Macedon spent his life wandering the world in search of the water of life. While both Alexander and his guide Khidr (see below) arrived at the well or fountain, Khidr was granted the ability to actually find the water, and drank it, becoming immortal. Alexander was not granted that reward.

       Khidr, a mysterious servant of God in the Qur'an, was a companion and teacher of Moses (Sura 18:65). Although invisible, Khidr is often present to assist, to teach, or to initiate a disciple, and is an important figure in Islamic mystical circles.

10   Representational art was forbidden by Islamic law because it distracted the faithful and tempted them into idolatry. Of all representational art, Chinese paintings and portraits were considered the most beautiful and intricate, and therefore the most dangerous.

11   While beautiful and distracting, paintings and images are lifeless and have no divine essence.

12, 13   These may be references to one of Háfiz's patrons, but may also allude to the martyred mystic Halláj, see notes to Ghazal 33.

GHAZAL 49

Meter: --o -o-o o--o -o-
Mudári' akhrab makfúf mahdhúf

Bayt

1   Among commentators there is debate as to the meaning of the first *misrá'* of this ghazal. The arrival of the festival of the lesser *'íd* (that marks the beginning of the lunar month of Shawwál and the end of Ramadan, the month of fasting) coincides with the

withering of the last rose. After a month of fasting one can drink wine again.

The end of Ramadan is signaled by the arrival of the new moon. The fast is decreed to be over when the slightest sliver of new moon is detected by the religious authorities.

In the Persian tradition, what one sees directly after one's first look at a new moon is of tremendous importance and should be auspicious. One should gaze at a new moon and then try to have one's eyes fall directly on the object of one's desire, perhaps one's beloved, or something of similar beauty. Here, in the second *misrá'*, one can read the beloved's face as a/the new moon, or one can read the *misrá'* as instructing the saqi to look at the wine or the friend's face after looking at the moon, or to look from the friend's face to the wine (and what's reflected in it).

2   The *himma* (see notes to Ghazal 12), the spiritual power or ambition, of those who kept the fast has extended the time of spring and roses beyond its customary limits.

3   In the first *misrá* "*ze mastí*" can mean either "ask, [while] drunk" or "ask a drunk."

      Jamshid, see notes to Ghazal 22.

5   *sahúr* is the (usually large) meal eaten just before first light, to fortify oneself for the upcoming day-long fast. The fast goes from first light until sunset.

8   The "royal pearl" referred to here is, of course, Hafez's poetry.

9   *pardah púshí*, to cover discreetly from the eyes of others; to overlook is one of God's attributes. This *bayt* could refer to a king/patron or to God.

GHAZAL 50
Meter: oo--/-o-- oo-- oo-- oo-/--
        Ramal sálim makhbún mahdhúf

Bayt

5   *raqíb*, rival, guardian. See notes to Ghazal 29.

6   '*ayyár*, translated here as "savvy," has a variety of meanings difficult to capture in English. See notes to Ghazal 10.

9   The cup of wine reflects one's own face, and that face is a creation

of God's and therefore is the essence of God, and God is the ultimate beloved. See also notes to Ghazal 33.

GHAZAL 51
Meter: oo--/-o-- oo-- oo-- oo-/--
Ramal sálim makhbún mahdhúf

Bayt

1   This *bayt* suggests the state of *faná'*, "annihilation," See notes to Ghazal 20.
4   Háfiz's heart burns with such intensity that it overwhelms and extinguishes the fires of the major Zoroastrian fire temple in southern Iran. His eyes cry such a volume of tears that the river Tigris is embarrassed.

GHAZAL 52
Meter: o-o- oo-- o-o- --
Mujtathth makhbún aslam

Bayt

1-2 The Persian word *keshtí*, means both "ship" and a drinking cup shaped like a ship. Háfiz's wordplay uses the former meaning in the first *misrá'* of *bayt* 1, and the latter in the first *misrá'* of *bayt* 2.
2   Legend, and the poet Sa'adi, tell of a man trapped on a sandbar in a river. A man upstream was casting bread into the water, and this bread, drifting down the river, kept the marooned man alive until he could be brought to safety. The tale affirms that truly good deeds are done unconditionally, without thought of acknowledgement or reward.
4   Rosewater is the favored libation at funerals, celebrations, and other religious gatherings. Here, the heretical wine is so favored that the rosewater is consumed with jealousy.
7   While in modern times wine is aged in wooden casks, in Háfiz's day it was aged in large ceramic amphorae.

GHAZAL 53
Meter: -o-- oo-- oo-- oo-/--
Ramal sálim makhbún mahdhúf

Bayt

1   According to Sharia' law, to eat or drink from anything made of gold is *harám*, forbidden. As is, of course, the drinking of alcohol. Háfiz is flaunting a double sin in this first *misra'*.

2   The "valley of the silent" is a cemetery.

3   Literal translation: "O cypress, by/on your green head, when I become dust/when I am buried, put aside coquetry/flirtation and cast your shade over this dust." Dust here is both the grave, and also the dust from which God made Adam.

5   Literal translation: "My heart that was bitter/wounded by the snake of the tip of your lock of hair,//send it to the healing house/hospital of antidote/remedy by means of your lips."

7   *bar án pák*, "at that pure one," can refer to the beloved, but also to the Qur'an. Before touching or looking into the Quar'an one must purify oneself with ritual ablutions.

9   The covering of the rosebud is its shirt. As it opens in love it rips its shirt.

GHAZAL 54

Meter: -o-- oo-- oo-- oo-/--
         Ramal sálim makhbún mahdhúf

In this ghazal, as throughout the *Díwán,* the word *má* can be translated as "I/me" or as "we/us."

Bayt

3   *deyr-i mughán*, see notes to Ghazal 2.
4   *ishárat*, see notes to Ghazal 10.
7   *kawn-o makán*, see notes to Ghazal 20.

GHAZAL 55

Meter: -o-- oo-- oo-- oo-/--
         Ramal sálim makhbún mahdhúf

Bayt

5   *nargis*, see notes to Ghazal 14.
7   Háfiz assumes that the great orb of heaven would not be subject to the afflictions described in the preceding *bayt*s. Upon inquiring,

he learns that even the orb of heaven suffers the same blows, pain, and abrupt changes in direction that the polo ball receives from the curved mallet. Polo was a popular courtly sport, and the mallet was sometimes used as an image for the beloved's curls, in which the lover's head has been caught.

GHAZAL 56

Meter: o-o- oo-- o-o- oo-/--
        Mujtathth makhbún mahdhúf

Bayt

1   The "voice of the invisible" is that of a heavenly angel or messenger, often Gabriel.
    Sháh Shujá's father, Mubariz ud-Dín Muhammad, had enforced Islamic law ruthlessly during his reign. (See Translators' Introduction, p. xix).

4   The *muhtasib* was an official charged with enforcing religious law. It was also an epithet used to refer to Mubariz al-Dín Muhammad.
    Núshanúsh is the Persian equivalent of "Cheers!" or "Skol!", meaning "may it be delightful!"

5   It appears that times have changed so dramatically that the local religious leader—a man so concerned about purity that he carried his prayer mat with him everywhere lest it touch the ground—got so drunk they had to carry him home on their shoulders.

7   Literal translation of this *bayt*: "The enlightened mind of the king is the place of the light of divine manifestation (*tajallí*). /If you seek to be near him, purify your intention." See also notes to Ghazal 35.

GHAZAL 57

Meter: -o-- -o-- -o-- -o-
        Ramal mahdhúf

Bayt

3   *zuhrah*, Venus, see notes to Ghazal 27.
    núsh, "Drink!" in the second *misrá'* can be read either as an imperative or as an exclamation ("Cheers!").

4	*zakhmí rasídan* means both "to be struck/receive a blow/wound" as a person and "to be struck" as a string on a musical instrument.
5	"You will not hear a secret *zín pardah*," meaning both "from this fret/mode, i.e. in this music or melody" and "within/from (inside) the veil. See notes to Ghazal 48.
6	Generally *hadith* means a saying, maxim, story, or piece of advice. It can also mean a divine saying or story of God or the Prophet. Here it may set up a resonance with the paraphrase, in the following *bayt*, of a famous *hadith qudsí* (a divine revelation that is not contained in the Qur'an).
7	This *bayt* paraphrases and refers to a *hadith qudsí* which describes a form of the station of *qurb*, "proximity" (see notes to Ghazal 26). *Qurb* is achieved by performing more than the ordinary acts of devotion. Schimmel quotes God's words from Abu Nasr as-Sarráj: "My servant ceases not to draw nigh unto me by works of devotion, until I love him, and when I love him I am the eye by which he sees and the ear by which he hears." Schimmel *Mystical Dimensions of Islam*, 133.
8	Literally *basát* means "on the blanket," as then and now vendors display their wares on blankets in the square or along the side of a road. It can also refer to the fabric on which food is placed and from which people eat (*sofreh*).
9	A literal translation of the first *misrá*: "O saqi, give wine, for he (Ásaf, identified in the second *misrá*) understood the rend-like behaviors and actions of Háfiz."

GHAZAL 58

Meter: o-o- oo-- o-o- --
        Mujtathth makhbún aslam

Bayt

6	This *bayt* is entirely in Arabic.

GHAZAL 59

Meter: -o-- oo-- oo-- oo-/--
        Ramal sálim makhbún mahdhúf

Bayt

1. The poet is free of attachment, hence free of both this world and the next.
2. The "snare-place of the phenomenal world," in contrast to heaven's garden.
4. *túbá*, see notes to Ghazal 20.

    Kawthar, see notes to Ghazal 17.

    The second *misrá'* means both "with the breeze/air of the head of your alleyway" and "with desire/longing for the head of your alleyway."
5. *lawh* means both the tablet or slate on which one writes and also the tablet of a tombstone.

    alif, the first letter of the Persian and Arabic alphabets, and also of the name Alláh. It also serves as the numeral "1" (its value in Islamic numerology), and to all Muslim mystics signifies the oneness and unity of God. It also suggests the tall and willowy figure of the beloved.
8. In the first *misrá'* Háfiz explains that his eyes have grown red from crying, and the red tears he sheds now are draining the blood from his heart.

GHAZAL 60

Meter: -o-- oo-- oo-- --
Ramal sálim makhbún mahdhúf

This ghazal is the one inscribed on Háfiz's tomb in Shiraz.

GHAZAL 61

Meter: o-o- oo-- o-o- oo-/--
Mujtathth makhbún aslam

Bayt

5. Musk, then as now a rare and precious commodity, is found in the musk-sac or musk-gland of the male musk deer, native to the Himalaya and Central Asia. Ancient Khotan, near the present-day city of Hotan in Xinjiang province, was said to produce the finest musk. The accumulation of the substance in the sack

apparently creates a burning pain for the animal. So, like the lover's joy, it is at once both precious and painful.

GHAZAL 62
Meter: -o-- oo-- oo-- --
Ramal sálim makhbún mahdhúf

Bayt

2 A caravan of pilgrims making the Hajj to Mecca were led by a holy man appointed by the government. Háfiz points out that such a man will see only the shell of faith (the Ka'aba), whereas Háfiz, as we learned in *bayt* 1, has seen its essence without leaving Shiraz.

GHAZAL 63
Meter: -o-- oo-- oo-- oo-/--
Ramal sálim makhbún mahdhúf

Tradition says that Háfiz composed this ghazal in Yazd, far from his beloved Shiraz, and was struggling with various difficulties. He longed desperately to return to home. The "ruined house" in the first *bayt* could refer to the city of Yazd, but can also be read as a metaphor for the material world. (Bargnaysi, 496.)

Bayt

2 The poet understands that as long as he is not one of the beloved's intimates, he will wander aimlessly and never reach his goal. Nevertheless, he chooses to follow the beloved's scent.

4 *wahshat*, a stage in the mystical path that is characterized by "a feeling of loneliness, of being far from intimacy, lost in the wilderness." See Schimmel, *Mystical Dimensions*, 132.

   The prison of Alexander (said to be the city of Yazd, and unrelated to Alexander the Great) serves as an image of the confines of this earthly life, in contrast to the kingdom of Solomon (here, Shiraz).

5 The untranslatable pun in the second *misrá'* plays with the pen image in the first: the "torn or wounded heart" means also the

split quill that forms the point of the pen, and the "crying eye" means the small well at the head of the quill's split that holds the ink after the pen is dipped in ink.

8   *tázíyán*, those who travel quickly and lightly, on horseback, also means Arabs or Arab horses. *pársáyán*, those who are saintly or abstemious, can also mean Persians.

9   Ásaf, see notes to Ghazal 15. Here, Háfiz is most likely referring to Jalal al-din Turanshah. (Bargnaysi, 497.) Like Qavam ud-Dín, Turanshah was one of Sháh Shuja's ministers, serving from 1369 CE until Shuja's death in 1384. (Limbert, *Shiraz in the Age of Hafez*, 78.)

GHAZAL 64

Meter: -o-- oo-- oo-- oo-/--
Ramal sálim makhbún mahdhúf

Bayt

1   *fatwá*, the sentence or ruling issued by a religious judge, it carries the force of a ruling made by God.

9   *ma'rifa*, gnosis, intuitive or divinely-inspired (as opposed to rational) understanding of God, is one of the highest stations of the mystical path. An *'arif* is the mystic who has reached this advanced station. See notes to Ghazal 4.

10   Adam is often, as here, a symbol for all mankind.

GHAZAL 65

Meter: -o-- -o-- -o-
Ramal mahdhúf

Commentaries suggest that this ghazal was composed by Háfiz after a quarrel with a king or patron.

Bayt

3   In Arabic, *má jará* means "whatever happened" and refers to an argument between two people. When a quarrel arose between two dervishes, members of the *kháneghán* (Sufi brotherhood) would sit in a circle and the quarreling dervishes would each reiterate their view of the problem in a calm voice. When the verdict was

announced, the "loser" would have to take off his cloak and stand in the antechamber or forecourt, where people's shoes were kept. In this *bayt* we have *má jará há*, the plural of the word, meaning "a lot of trouble."

GHAZAL 66
Meter: o-o- oo-- o-o- --
Mujtathth makhbún aslam

Bayt
2   The commentaries debate the meaning of the first *misrá*, citing other poets who describe holier-than-thou clerics that use the proceeds from their mosque to buy alcohol. *vajh* means both "face/demeanor" and "cash." *khomár* usually means "hungover" but can also describe languid quality of the beloved's eyes. *neshastan* can mean "to subside" as well as "to sit." Therefore, one could translate the first *misrá*' as "The grim expression of the ascetic will not subside/go away by obtaining the cash for his drinking."
5   *khánegháh*, the eastern Islamic world this was a center of Sufi activity, where Sufis lived and practiced.
9   *fatwa'*, see notes to Ghazal 64.

GHAZAL 67
Meter: -o-- oo-- oo-- oo-/--
Ramal sálim makhbún mahdhúf

Bayt
2   To teach a parrot to speak, the bird is placed in front of a mirror. From behind the mirror the trainer speaks the words he wants the parrot to say. The bird, thinking it is its reflection speaking, mimics the words back. Here Háfiz adds another layer to the image: Háfiz, the man behind the mirror, is himself saying only what God, the "first teacher," has taught him to say.
5   Literal translation of this *bayt*: "Although (drinking) ruby wine is wrong with a multi-colored coat/do not blame me because I wash away from it the color of hypocrisy." The coat of the dreg-drinking indigent rend is colorful because it has been patched many times with different kinds of fabric.

6   This *bayt* also implies that all that is and occurs is God's will.
7   Musk from Khotan. See notes to Ghazal 61.

GHAZAL 68
Meter: -o-- o-o- oo-
Khafíf sálim makhbún

Commentaries suggest that this ghazal refers to Sháh Mansúr (b. 750 AH, 1349 CE), nephew of Sháh Shujá', and the last of the Muzzafarids, who died fighting against Timur in 795 AH/1392 CE. Háfiz lived for the first two years of Mansúr's reign, and mentions him admiringly in nine ghazals.

Bayt
2   Robes and cloaks lacked pockets, so things kept on one's person were carried inside one's sleeve.
9   We read this as an allusion to the colored banners carried into battle. The red lion suggests bravery, the black viper a deadly lack of color.

GHAZAL 69
Meter: o-o- oo-- o-o- oo-/--
Hazaj mahdhúf

In this ghazal, Háfiz rails against the orthodox Sufi orders (see notes to Ghazal 4) whom he compares (unfavorably) with the rends.

GHAZAL 70
Meter: o-o- oo-- o-o- oo-/--
Mujtathth makhbún mahdhuf—

GHAZAL 71
Meter: --o -o-o o--o -o-
Mudári' akhrab makfúf mahdhúf

Bayt
3   Literal translation of the *bayt*: "The sun of wine rose in the East of the cup./If you seek the provisions/necessities of happiness, give up sleeping."

4	Wine was stored in amphorae and served in jugs which were, like Adam, made from clay. In Persian the word for "skull" is a compound word, literally "the cup of my head." See notes to Ghazal 45.

GHAZAL 72
Meter: -o-- -o-- -o-- -o-
Ramal mahdhúf

Bayt

5	When it is extinguished or snuffed out, the candle dies, but with the coming of daylight the loss of the candle's light doesn't matter.
6	A reference to the stories of Farhad's doomed love for Shirin. See notes to Ghazal 45. *shírín* also means "sweet."

GHAZAL 73
Meter: o--- I--- o---
Hazaj mahdhúf

Bayt

5	*sib-i zanakh*, the "apple of the chin," see notes to Ghazal 2.
8	*pír* (and its plural, *pírán*) can mean simply "elder" or "old one," or refer to a spiritual master (see notes to Ghazal 1), or, as here, imply both.
9	*arghawán*, the redbud or Judas-tree, whose deep red blossoms look like the heartblood of lovers.
10	The Zindehrúd, literally "river of life," is the river that runs through the center of Isfahan. Ironically, it has dried up in recent years and over four hundred villages, dependent on it for irrigation, have been abandoned.

GHAZAL 74
Meter: -o-- oo-- oo-- oo-/--
Ramal sálim makhbún mahdhúf

Much of the imagery here refers to or suggests the ritual ablutions required by the *sharí'a*. One must perform ablutions before entering a mosque, after menstruation, or after sexual or other unclean activity.

Bayt

1   *dúsh*, see notes to Ghazal 33.

GHAZAL 75

Meter: o--- o--- o--
Hazaj mahdhúf

Bayt

1   *chagháneh* can refer to handheld percussion instruments of various kinds, often a gourd filled with small stones or seeds.

5   Literal translation of this *bayt*: "You will not profit, like a belt, from that waist/if you see yourself in the middle." We interpret this *bayt* as follows: according to the aesthetics of classical poetry, the waist of the beautiful beloved must be tiny. If you wish to embrace her/him, diminish your ego to that tiny scale. Here Háfiz goes one step further: if you wish to embrace the beloved, efface yourself into non-existence.

6   The *anqá*, or Simurgh, is a mythical bird, see notes to Ghazal 4.

7   Literal translation of second *misrá'*: "The thought of water and soil on the road is just an excuse." Adam, the first man, was made from soil and water. According to hadith, "God created man to reflect his own beauty in him," but, of course, nothing exists but God.

GHAZAL 76

Meter: --o -o-- --o -o--
Mudári' akhrab sálim

Bayt

1   In various editions of Háfiz's *Diwán* there are material variations in the text and order of the *bayts* in this ghazal. Instead of following Khanlari here, we have followed Khorramshahi, Qazvini and Sayeh.

GHAZAL 77

Meter: o-o- oo-- o-o- oo-/--
Mujtathth makhbún mahdhúf

In this ghazal, Háfiz speaks of Timur's (Tamerlane's) destruction of Persian cities.

Bayt

7   The *simoom*, "poison wind," is a hot, dry, dust-laden desert wind that blows in the Sahara and the Arabian Peninsula.

8   In this *bayt*, Háfiz compares the city of Shiraz to the precious gem that was the seal of Solomon. Like the philosopher's stone, the seal had extraordinary powers. Ahriman, the god of darkness in Zoroastrianism, is seen as a devil.

9   This *bayt* suggests that perhaps wise men of the west or east might have a solution.

GHAZAL 78
Meter: --o o--- --o o---
Hazaj akhrab sálim

Bayt

4   The *záhid*'s behavior has been inconsistent with his outwardly pious demeanor, and consistent with the contents of a sensuous song.
    rabab, see notes to Ghazal 2.

5   *bí sar-o pá* can mean "insolent, nasty, mean," in the manner of a low-life or punk; it can also mean "without beginning or end."

6   In the second *misrá'*, *táb* is used twice, playing on its meanings of "a twist or curl" and "a glow or burning."

GHAZAL 79
Meter: --o o-o- o--o -o-
Mudári' akhrab makfúf mahdhúf

Bayt

2   The second *misrá'* can also be read as "for one day you will become a father."

3   *wujúd*, "existence," usually refers to the existence of God into which the mystic is dissolved at the stage of *faná'* (see notes to Ghazal 20). Here it suggests earthly existence, or attachment to the material world.

7	Literal translation on the second *misra'*: "when on the road of the Possessor-of-Glory (a name or attribute of God) you lose head and foot (you become nothing)."
9	*zír-o zabar*, literally "under and over," refers to the "overturning of hearts" that will occur at the Resurrection. One whose heart is free of attachment to the world is already in a state of union with God, and will be unaffected.

GHAZAL 80

Meter: -o-- oo-- oo-- oo-/--
Ramal sálim makhbún mahdhúf

Bayt

1	*daftar*, see notes to Ghazal 41.
5	The Persian word *keshtí* means both "ship" and a drinking cup shaped like a ship. Similar wordplay also appears in Ghazals 52 and 75.
6	The flame is the candle's tongue. The moth, drawn irresistibly to the flame, is too distracted to speak.
7	The narcissus may imagine it resembles the eyes of the beloved, but the wise ones know that the narcissus cannot see.
10	*fardá* can mean "tomorrow" or "the Day of Resurrection."

SELECTED BIBLIOGRAPHY

PERSIAN EDITIONS OF THE DIWAN-I HÁFIZ

Háfiz-i Shirazi, Shams ud-Din Muhammad (d. 1389):

Diwan-i Shams ud-Din Muhammad Háfiz-i Shirazi. Edited by N. Ahmad and S. M. R. J. Nai'ini. Tehran: Amir Kabir, 1971.

Diwan-i Khwajah Háfiz-i Shirazi. Edited by A. Anjavi Shirazi. Second edition. Tehran: 'Elmi, 1967.

Diwan-i Háfiz Edited by P. N. Khanlari. Tehran: Khwarazmi, 1980.

Diwan-i Háfiz. Edited by H. Pizhman. Tehran: Beroukhim, 1939.

Diwan-i Shams ud-Din Muhammad Háfiz-i Shirazi. Edited by M. Qazvini and Q. Ghani. Tehran: Zavvar, 1941.

Diwan-i Hafez. Based on a newly discovered manuscript written around the time of Hafez. Eds. Sayyed Sadeq Sajjadi & Ali Bahramiyan with notes and commentary by Kazem Bargnaysi. Tehran: Fekr-i rouz, 2001.

Hafiz beh Saay-e Sayeh/Háfiz. Edited by H. E. Sayeh. Tehran: Karnameh, 1999.

SELECTED TRANSLATIONS

Arberry, A. J. *Fifty Poems of Háfiz*. Cambridge: The University Press, 1947.

Avery, Peter and John Heath-Stubbs. *Thirty Poems*. London: Murray, 1952.

Bell, Gertrude. *Poems from the Divan of Háfiz*. London: W. Heinemann, 1928.

Bicknell, Herman. *Háfiz of Shiraz*. London: Tubner and Co, 1875.

Bly, Robert and Leonard Lewisohn. *The Angels Knocking on the Tavern Door*. New York City: Harper Perennial, 2009.

Boylan, Michael. *Hafez: Dance of Life*. Washington, D.C.: Mage, 1988.

Clarke, H. Wilberforce. The Divan-i Háfiz. Cambridge: The University Press, 1891. Reprinted, New York: Samuel Weiser, Inc., 1970.

Cloutier, David. *News of Love: Poems of Separation and Unions by Háfiz of Shiraz*. Greensboro: Unicorn Press, 1984.

Crowe, Thomas Rain. *Drunk on the Wine of the Beloved: 100 Poems of Háfiz*. Boston: Shambala, 2001.

Davis, Dick. *Faces of Love: Hafez and the Poets of Shiraz*. 2012. New York: Penguin, 2013.

Leaf, Walter. *Versions from Háfiz*. London: G. Richards, 1898.

La Galienne, Richard. *Odes from the Divan of Háfiz*. London: Duckworth and Co., 1905.

Nott, John. Select Odes from the Persian Poet Hafez. London: T Cadell, 1787.

Payne, John. *The Poems of Shemseddin Mohammed Háfiz of Shiraz*. London: Villon Society, privately published, 1901.

Persia Society of London. *Selections from the Rubaiyat and Odes of Háfiz.* London: J.M. Watkins, 1920.

Squires, Geoffrey. *Hafez: Translations and Interpretations of the Ghazals.* Oxford, OH: Miami University Press, 2014.

PUBLISHED WORKS IN EUROPEAN AND PERSIAN LANGUAGES

Andrews, Walter G. *Poetry's Voice, Society's Song: Ottoman Lyric Poetry.* Seattle: University of Washington Press, 1985.

Arberry, A. J. "The Art of Háfiz." In *Aspects of Islamic Civilization as Depicted in the Original Texts.* London: George Allen & Unwin, 1964: 344-58,

———. "Háfiz and His English Translators." *Islamic Culture,* 20 (1946): 111-128 and 229-49.

———. "Orient Pearls at Random Strung." *Bulletin of the School of Oriental and African Studies* 11 (1943-1946): 699-712.

———. "Three Persian Poems." *Iran,* 2 (1964): 1-12.

Ashouri, Dariyoush, *Erfan va Rendi dar Sher-i Hafez* (14th edition). Tehran: Nashr-i Markaz. 2017.

Brookshaw, Dominic. *Háfiz and His Contemporaries: Poetry, Performance and Patronage in Fourteenth Century Iran.* British Institute of Persian Studies. London: I. B. Tauris, 2019.

Bausani, Alessandro. "Ghazal." *Encyclopedia of Islam (New Edition).* Edited by B. Lewis, V. L. Menage et al., ed. London: Luzac and Co., 1971.

Boyce, Mary. "A Novel Interpretation of Háfiz." *Bulletin of the School of Oriental and African Studies* 15 (1953): 279-88.

"Browne, Edward G. *A Literary History of Persia*, 4 Vols. Cambridge: The University Press, 1920. Reprinted, 1969.

Chittick, William C. *The Sufi Path of Knowledge*. Albany, NY: SUNY Press. 1989.

———. *The Sufi Path of Love*. Albany, NY: SUNY Press, 1985.

Hillman, Michael. "Háfiz and Poetic Unity through Verse Rhythms." *Journal of Near Eastern Studies* 31 (1972): 1-10.

———. *Iranian Culture: A Persianist View*. Lanham, MD: University Press of America, 1990.

———. "Sound and Sense in a *Ghazal* of Háfiz." The Muslim World 61.2 (1971): 112-21.

———. *Unity in the Ghazals of Háfiz*. Studies in Middle Eastern Literatures, No. 6. Minneapolis and Chicago. Bibiliotheca Islamica, 1976.

Hodgson, Marshall G. S. *The Venture of Islam*, 3 vols. Chicago: University of Chicago Press, 1974.

Khurramshahi, Baha'al Din. *Háfiz-Nameh*. Tehran: Surush, 1987.

———. *Dhihn wa Zaban-i Háfiz*. Tehran, 1982, 1989.

Limbert, John W. *Shiraz in the Age of Hafez: The Glory of a Medieval Persian City*. Seattle: University of Washington Press, 2004.

Lewisohn, Leonard, Editor. *Háfiz and the Religion of Love in Classical Persian Poetry*. London: I. B. Tauris, 2015.

Meisami, Julie Scott. "Allegorical Gardens in the Persian Poetic Tradition." *International Journal of Middle East Studies* 17 (1985): 229-60.

———. "Allegorical Techniques in the Ghazals of Háfiz." *Edebiyat* 4.1 (1979): 1-40.

———. "The Analogical Structure of Persian Courtly Lyric: Háfiz's 81st Ghazal." Paper Presented at the Nineteenth International Congress on Medieval Studies, Kalamazoo, Michigan, May 1984.

———. *Medieval Persian Court Poetry*. Princeton, NJ: Princeton University Press, 1986.

———. The World's Pleasure: Háfiz's Allegorical Gardens." *Comparative Criticism* No. 5 (1983): 153-85.

———. "Norms and Conventions of the Classical Persian Lyric: A Comparative Approach to the Ghazal." *Proceedings of the 9th Congress of the International Comparative Literature Association*. Innsbruck, 1979, vol. 1.

———. "Sir William Jones and the Reception of Persian Literature." *South Asian Review* 8.5 (1984): 61-70.

Nategh, Homa. *Khonyagari, Mey va Shadi Háfiz-i Shirazi*. Los Angeles: Sherekat-i Ketab. 2004.

Pursglove, Parvin. "Translations of Háfiz and Their Influence on English Poetry since 1771: A Study and Critical Bibliography." PhD thesis, University College of Swansea, Wales, 1983.

Raja'i, Ahmad 'Ali. *Farhang-i Ash'ar-i Háfiz*, Vol. 1. Tehran: Zavvar, 1961.

Rehder, Robert M. "The Text of Háfiz." *Journal of the American Oriental Society* 94 (1974): 145-56.

———. "New Material for the Text of Háfiz." *Iran* 3 (1965).

———. "The Unity of the Ghazals of Háfiz" *Der Islam* 51 (1974): 55-96.

Rypka, Jan, and others. *History of Iranian Literature.* Edited by Karl Jahn. Dordecht, Holland: D. Reidel, 1968.

Schimmel, Annemarie. *As Through a Veil: Mystical Poetry in Islam.* New York: Columbia University Press, 1982.

———. "Háfiz and His Critics," *Studies in Islam* 16 (1979): 1-33.

———. *Mystical Dimensions of Islam.* Chapel Hill, NC: University of North Carolina Press, 1975.

———. "Persian Poetical Symbolism." Mimeographed. Cambridge, MA: Harvard University, 1979.

———. *A Two-Colored Brocade: The Imagery of Persian Poetry.* Chapel Hill, NC: University of North Carolina Press, 1992.

Schroeder, Eric. "Verse Translation and Háfiz" *Journal of Near Eastern Studies* 7 (1947): 209-22.

———. "The Wild Deer Mathnawi." *Journal of Aesthetics and Art Criticism* 11 (1952): 118-34.

Sells, Michael A., transl. *Desert Tracings: Six Classic Arabian Odes by 'Alqama, Shanfara, Labid, 'Antara, Al-A'sha, and Dhu al-Rumma.* Middletown, CT: Wesleyan University Press, 1989.

Stetkevych, Suzanne. Editor. *Reorientations: Studies in Arabic and Persian Poetics.* Bloomington, IN: Indiana University Press, 1993.

Sudi, Busnavi. *Sharh-i Sudi bar Háfiz.* Translated by 'Esmaat Sattarzadeh. 3rd printing, 4 vols. Tehran: Rangin, 1969.

Wickens, G. M. "An Analysis of Primary and Secondary Significations in the Third Ghazal of Háfiz." *Bulletin of the School of Oriental and African Studies* 14 (1952): 627-38.

———. "Haafiz" *Encyclopedia of Islam* (New Edition), 1971.

———. "The Persian Conception of Artistic Unity and Its Implications in Other fields." *Bulletin of the School of Oriental and African Studies* 14 (1952): 239-43.

Yarshater, Ehsan. "The Theme of Wine Drinking and the Concept of the Beloved in Early Persian Poetry." *Studia Islamica* 13 (1960): 43-53.

———. "Persian Poetry in the Timurid and Safavid Periods." *The Cambridge History of Iran*, vol. 6. Cambridge, MA: The University Press, 1986.

Yousofi, Gholam Hosein. "Colors in the Poetry of Háfiz." *Edebiyat* 2:2 (1977): 15-28.

ABOUT THE TRANSLATORS

Elizabeth T. Gray, Jr. is a poet, translator, and corporate consultant. Her translated selection of poems by Iran's iconic woman poet Forough Farrokhzad (1934-1967), *Let Us Believe in the Beginning of the Cold Season* (New Directions) was a finalist for the 2023 PEN Prize for Poetry in Translation. Her books of poetry include the long poem, *Salient* (New Directions), and the sequence of poems, *Series | India* (Four Way Books). Her work has also appeared in *The Paris Review, Modern Poetry in Translation, Poetry International, Dispatches from the Poetry Wars, Hyperallergic, Little Star, Talisman, The Harvard Review, The New England Review, Antaeus, The Kenyon Review,* and elsewhere. She has served as guest editor of *Epiphany* and *The New Haven Review.* Gray was also the founding CEO and managing partner of Conflict Management, Inc. and Alliance Management Partners, LLC. She serves on the boards of *The Beloit Poetry Journal*, Kimbilio Fiction, Friends of Writers, and the Abdorrahman Boroumand Center for Human Rights in Iran, and from 2009-2015 served as chair of the board of the Iran Human Rights Documentation Center. She holds a BA and JD from Harvard University and MFA from the Program for Writers at Warren Wilson College. She lives in New York City. www.etgrayjr.com.

Iraj Anvar is an actor, singer, stage and film director, writer, translator, and educator. He completed his first diploma in Genoa, Italy at the Swiss School, then gained a degree in acting and directing at Alessandro Fersen's Studio di Arti Sceniche in Rome, Italy. On returning to his native Tehran, he co-founded the Tehran Theater Workshop. He directed and performed in many stage and television productions, and translated plays and film dialogue into Persian, including plays he directed for the stage. He also taught acting and diction at Tehran University. A few months before the 1979 Islamic Revolution, Anvar moved to New York City, where he received his PhD in Middle Eastern and Islamic Studies at NYU, where he taught Persian language and literature for several years. He directed *From Kaf Mountain to Vernon* (2002), a documentary film about an Abkazanian community in Vernon, British Columbia, and published his translations of works by Genet, Pirandello, Adamov, and others in Iran. In addition to his collaborations with Elizabeth T. Gray, Jr., he created the English subtitles for the Oscar-nominated film, *Children of Heaven* (1998). He has taught Persian literature and language at Harvard, Columbia, the University of Pennsylvania, New York University, and the University of Wisconsin. In 2008, he established a Persian program at Brown University, where he also taught a course on Iranian cinema. He has had a lifelong involvement in the poetry of Rumi, Háfiz, and Ferdowsi. In New York, he has read and sung Rumi, Háfiz, and other classical poets in Persian and in his own translations at the Asia Society, Cathedral of St. John the Divine, St. Bartholomew's Church, the Long House Preserve Garden, the Bowery Poetry Club, Stony Brook and New York Universities, and several other institutions. His translations of Rumi ghazals include *Divan-i Shams-i Tabriz, Forty eight ghazals,* (Semar) and *Rumi: Say Nothing* (Morning Light Press). A third set of Rumi's poetry in English translation, *Birds of Wonder,* is forthcoming.

www.ingramcontent.com/pod-product-compliance
Lightning Source LLC
Chambersburg PA
CBHW030040240426
43667CB00035B/176